The Flute

The Flute

Selected Poems of

Rabindranath Tagore

Translated by

Jadu Saha

SHIPRA

ISBN: 81-7541-144-9

First Published in India in 2003

11 Weatherwood Cresc.,
Ottawa, ON K2E 7C5, Canada

Published by:
SHIPRA PUBLICATIONS
115-A, Vikas Marg, Shakarpur,
Delhi-110092 (India)
Ph: 22458662, 22500954 Fax: 91-11-22458662
Email : siprapub@satyam.net.in
www.shiprapublications.com

Laser Typeset by:
Sunshine Graphics
Delhi-110032

Printed at:
Chaudhary Offset Process
Delhi-110051

Dedicated to

Sanat Chatterji, Uttarpara
Subal Chandara Saha, Kolkata
Nandlal Jagdeo, Ottawa
Otto Cepella, Ottawa

and

To the memory of
Ajay Dixit

Acknowledgements

As always my friend Ruth Latta has made many suggestions for improvement while editing the manuscript. I am indebted to her. Ms. Indrani Sinha of New Delhi has made valuable contributions by making many comments and suggestions while comparing the translations with the original poems in Bengali. I thankfully acknowledge her painstaking editing of the manuscript.

Contents

Introduction

Rabindranath Tagore (1861-1941) was born into one of the wealthy and cultured families of Bengal. His life almost coincided with the direct British rule (the Raj) of India, starting two years after its beginning in 1859 and ending in 1941, only six years before the end of the Raj, in 1947. Rabindranath was the crown jewel of the Bengali Renaissance period, which was started by the great reformer Raja Rammohun Roy before the poet's birth and ended with the poet's death. He received many honours from India and around the world including the Nobel Prize in literature in 1913. He was the first non-European to receive it.

This Titan's life-long poetical literary output includes about two thousand five hundred songs, both the lyrics and music and an endless variety of outstanding and innovative poems, plays in verse and half a dozen musical ballets. His other literary works include three volumes of short stories, novels, plays in prose, essays on a wide variety of subjects, and memoirs and personal letters which were, in effect, *belles* letters. He gave numerous lectures in English and corresponded with friends who could not understand Bengali. Rabindranath translated some of his works, including the Nobel Prize winning poems, *Gitanjali.* The Sahitya Akademy of India published three volumes of "The English Writings of Rabindranath Tagore" in 1996. But most of the poet's works were in his mother tongue, Bengali. Even more than sixty years after the death of the poet, only a fraction of his work, including poetry, has been translated to English. So Rabindranath's poetical genius is practically unknown to the world at large. Alas, even within India he is mainly known as the poet of *Gitanjali*, which is a minor book; and the theme is but a small branch of the giant Banyan tree of his poetry.

In this book I present a collection of English translations of his poems in as close a rhyme as possible to the original Bengali.

Before engaging in a discussion of Rabindranath's poetical genius I wish to make a few general comments about the continuous onward movement of his poetry. Without keeping in mind the principal characteristics of his poetry, the true meaning and charm of any specific book or poem cannot be fully appreciated.

Rabindranath is a romantic poet and nothing but a poet. Since the romantic movement emerged in Britain and Germany in the 1790s, most of the romantic poets saw themselves as free spirits expressing their own imaginative truths. To them, art was not imitation or interpretation but creation in the most significant sense. Wordsworth defined poetry as 'the spontaneous overflow of powerful feelings', Coleridge remarked that all fine arts are a revelation of the inner world of man. Shelley defined poetry as the expression of imagination.

In Bengali literature Michael Madhusudan Dutta, Nabin Chandra Sen, Hemchandra Bandopadhyay and Biharilal Chakrabarty started the epoch of the romantic period in Bengali poetry. Rabindranath was greatly influenced by Biharilal in his early poetry writing. He was also influenced by the form, language and sound of "Vaishnav Padavali" at an early age as can be seen in his *Bhanu Singha Thakurer Padavali.* But this was the experimental phase of Rabindranath's poetry and is not considered typical of his style or voice.

In all his thoughts and works Rabindranath tried to give expression to his innermost feelings and personal experience. Whatever in this world touched his heart he gave expression to it, not by analytical reasoning or from any particular ideology, but from his inner feelings. It is this artistic and skilful expression of personal experience and emotion that is the hallmark of Rabindranath's poetry.

The principal driving force of the onward movement of Rabindranath's poetry is its humanism. No Indian poet since Kalidas in the fourth century A.D. wrote so much about man and Nature. European poetry is mainly concerned with mankind and Nature whereas Indian poetry is primarily about devotion to God. That is why European poetry has so much variety and complexity. Indian poetry is deep and intensely focussed within.

In this respect, Kalidas and Rabindranath are close to the Western mind and surprisingly divergent from the main flow of Indian poetry. But Western readers see him as a mystic, unlike themselves and poets of their tradition because they know him only as the poet of *Gitanjali*, in which he wrote about spiritual matters and about his Lord, friend and beloved. They did not have access to the poet's major poetical works, most of which he wrote after *Gitanjali*.

Rabindranath dearly loved this 'beautiful world' from his childhood. Wordsworth found the essence of the creation in nature and Rabindranath found the essence of man in nature. He realised that the beauty of the world is not as perfect and as pure as a hundred-petal lotus. As this realisation crystallised and became deep, his love for the world took a different form, which may be termed as 'hardened'. But there was never a hair-thin crack in it and he never turned his face from mankind and Nature.

Rabindranath tried to build the edifice of his poetry with diverse elements. Alas, it remained incomplete at the time of his death after sixty years of tireless effort. We can say that for the first fifty years of his poetic life from *'Sandhyasangit'* (Evening songs) to *'Mahua'* (Indian Butter Tree) his poems have been called 'romantic' and 'sweet'. It is true that many poems of this period reflect detachment, sadness and even bitterness. But the change in his poems during the last ten of his eighty years life is quite remarkable. Rabindranath has called this period his initiation to 'the tune of scorching sun', meaning writing about the unpleasant things in the world.

Nevertheless, the onward movement of his poetry never stopped. If there was a temporary pause and if he ever came back to the same place again it was like climbing a spiral staircase. He went up but never moved in a circle. Like a tropical forest he renewed himself and grew. More importantly, as we will see later, at every turn he surpassed himself. The only things that changed were the language and the style of expression.

Lastly, the form and sound of Rabindranath's poetry are lyrical, even those works written as 'prose poetry'. They all sing.

'Sandhyasangit' Phase (1882-86)

I have included *'Sandhyasangit'* (Evening Songs), *'Prabhatsangit'* (Morning Songs), *'Chabi O Gan'* (Picture and Song) and *'Kadi O Komal'* (Sharps and Flats) in this phase. Rabindranath himself considered 'Evening Songs' as the beginning of his poetical career. He did not think that the poems and ballets published before this period were his true voice or style. Not that these reached their perfection in this phase. That would happen later. This was the period of experimentation for him, strengthening the wings of the 'song-bird'. Most of the poems in this phase are more important for their historicity than for their sound and form.

The poems in *Sandhyasangit'* have a shadow of darkness about them. Kadambari Devi, Rabindranath's sister-in-law, had encouraged and supported the poet in his writing efforts from an early age. Her suicide at the age of twenty-six, drove the twenty-four year old poet into the darkness of grief over the loss of a close friend. So we see the poet self absorbed in '*Sandhyasangit*' and immersed in deep sorrow. The poem 'Dew-drop' (p. 43) is only one example.

About *'Sandhyasangit'* the poet said,

> "This time is most memorable to me in the history of my poetry writing. 'Sandhyasangit' may not have much value as poetry. Its poems are very unpolished. The only good thing about them is that all of a sudden one day I could write on my own whatever delighted me. The writing may not have value but the delight has."
>
> — *'Jibansmriti', Rabindra Rachanabali, Vol.10, p.93.* Translated by the author.

Certainly it has. It is in *'Sandhyasangit'* that the poet found his medium of expression, the lyric. Never before were the movements of his poetry so free and musical. The wings that carried him aloft in *'Sandhyasangit'* would later become strong and carry him all through his poetical career.

The naming of the next book as *'Prabhatsangit'*, Morning Songs, is significant. After the darkness of the evening came the arrival of a new dawn when the sunbeams entered the dark caves of his heart and melted the ice of sorrow. This is the awakening of Rabindranath to the beauty of the Creation and the awareness of his destiny as a poet. The poet has many times written about this awakening and about his sense of beauty:

> *"Never before had I observed such wonderfulness in the movement of people's limbs when they do even the simplest of tasks — now the lyric of this movement overwhelmed me every moment. I could not see them as individual parts but as a whole. In this moment everywhere in this world, in many places, in myriad of tasks and with many needs millions of people are bustling. I could see the movement of the worldwide human-body as one vast whole and I could glimpse the immense beauty of a great dance. * * * So long I saw the world with a detached look and for that reason I could not see it's ineffable whole face. One day when a beam of light emanating from the depth of my soul fell on the whole world I could no longer see that world as filled with events and matters. I saw it as one complete whole in its entirety. From this a feeling came to my mind that from the deepest cave of my heart a song was coming out and was returning to its source as an echo from all lands and time."*
>
> — *'Jibansmriti', Rabindra Rachanabali, Vol. 10, p. 101.*
>
> Translated by the author.

This is the event, this is the song of 'creative unity' that Rabindranath sang in the poem, 'Awakening of the Waterfall' (p.47) and he would sing of this unity in his many poems in the future.

In his next book, *Chabi O Gan* (Picture and Song), we find that the poet is more interested in painting pictures than singing songs. In other words, the form became more important than the sound. Even a simple sight like a girl walking alone through the meadow evoked an outpouring empathy for her and he painted that picture against a setting sun (p.51). We notice the sorrow in *'Sandhyasangit'* still casting its shadow in the poet's mind and the lyrical quality of the poem is less pronounced. Rabindranath said that if he had the skill he would have painted pictures in *'Chabi O Gan'* rather than writing poems.

In *'Kadi O Komal'* (Sharps and Flats) we find along with sorrow and emptiness another note making its presence. The poet himself, calling our attention to this note, said, "For the first time I said something that would appear as the heart of my future poems time again:

"From this lovely world I don't want to part
Among humanity I want to be living...."
(p.55)

Two opposite notes are playing simultaneously in the poems of this book. On the one hand the poet is singing about the triumph of life and on the other the personal realisation of the pain of death. In the first phase of Rabindranath's poetry we first find the tune of sorrow in *'Sandhyasangit'*, in the second book, *'Prabhatsangit'*, the tune of his exuberant embrace of the beautiful world. These two tunes playing simultaneously in the fourth book, *'Kadi O Komal.'*

Manashi (She who is in the Mind) and *Sonar Tari* **(The Golden Boat)** Phase (1890-94)

In "*Manashi*" (She who is the Mind) we find the movement of painting pictures and singing songs is progressing towards excellence. The only one poem in this selection from "*Manashi*" is a fine example of the poet's skill in painting pictures in words. The language has become little strong and the emotion a little controlled but neither yet quite mature.

To understand and appreciate *"Sonar Tari"* (The Golden Boat) one has to understand the impact of the river Padma on Rabindranath, his life and his poetry. The poet's family had substantial land holdings in East Bengal (now Bangladesh) of undivided India. The responsibility for managing the estate fell on Rabindranath. He spent months in a boathouse in this river. The Padma is like the soul of the eastern part of India and its people. She has intimate connection with the Ganges but their paths are different. To paraphrase one of the authorities on Rabindranath's literary works, Pramathanath Bishi (*Rabindrakabyaprabaha)* one can say that disregarding the traditions of India, this river, like unbridled imagination, is ever running in search of the unknown. There is something in its flow that can easily make the collective mind of the people of Bengal leave the age-old traditions of India behind and move forward. There is a streak of individuality in the minds of the people of Bengal and a strong impulse to cross the boundary of ancient thoughts. This impulse is so strong that it touched many aspects of life in Bengal. "India faces the past and Bengal faces the future," so said Bishi. Like the fast flowing Padma, fast movement dominates Rabindranath's poetry. It is on this Padma that the poet's poetry found its maturity. He came out of the haze that prevailed in him for so long, he found direct contact with people and his own innate nature, love for mankind and Nature. He wrote many personal letters describing the very many sights he saw and their impact on him.

> *"While observing the flow of the river the thought comes to me that if I want to separate the matter from the movement and want to envision the movement alone I can do that here by just concentrating only on the current of the river. There is stop and go at times in the movement of people and animals. But a river is ever moving, and for that reason I can find a similarity with our consciousness and us. Our bodies move our feet and other limbs part of the time but our mind is always moving. For this reason the Padma of the month of Bhadra' seems like a gigantic mental force. That force is breaking and shattering the banks and moving at will and expressing itself in a bewildering pattern of waves and murmuring songs. The fast moving current of the forward moving river is like our desires and the stationary land with its many crops are the objects of our desires."*
>
> — *Chinnapatra,* August 24, 1894. Translated by the author.

Later in life whenever the poet thought about the river he never hesitated to express his gratitude:

> *"I don't think I will ever forget even in my next birth the numerous occasions I received messages from the river's words."*
>
> —-*Bhanusingher Patravali,* No. 57. Translation by the author.

The main ingredients of Rabindranath's poetry are his love for mankind and the Earth. His keen interest and wonder in the life and beauty of Bengal and the mood of detachment that the natural sights in Bengal evoke in human mind — all of these had their beginning during the poet's stay on this Padma. Later in his life when he lived far away from the Padma, the river was always in his mind's eye and influenced his poetry. This is most noticeable in *Balaka.*

The first poem of the book, *'Sonar Tari'*, also titled the same, has some of these ingredients. This poem has been the subject of much discussion and interpretation. Some have even found deep philosophical and spiritual meaning in it. That is the nature of poetry by great poets. They speak to us at many levels and the poet himself does not always know what thought inspired him to write the poem.

As a poem, *'Sonar Tari'* (p. 60) is an excellent example of Rabindranath's artistry. The rumbling clouds, endless rain, fiercely flowing swollen river, the farmers busy in harvesting the paddy, boats filled with sheaves piled high, trees like ink-smears on the far bank — all of these create a natural unexpressed restlessness in the mind. Added to them is the sadness and loneliness of the rainy season. Together they create a sad mood in sensitive minds. This is perhaps what has been captured in this beautiful poem. It does not need any deeper meaning or philosophy.

In the introduction to the book *'Sonar Tari'* the poet wrote,

> *"All the branches of a tree do not spread in one direction and in the same way*** In this place (on the Padma) a communion with people was taking place in my life. The clamour of peoples' lives with their message of joy and sorrow touched my heart. My mind was awake to the close contact with people. I thought about them, worked for them, determined to do many duties and that determination is in my thoughts even now. It is the contact with people that is flowing side by side in my poetry and in my work and in my life."*

—*Rabindra Rachanabali*, Vol. 1, p. 342. Translated by the author.

Another painting of a rainy night on the shore of the Padma, and his thoughts about the loneliness of another person close to his heart, is in the third poem, 'On the Way to the River'. But in the second poem, "On the Doctrine of Maya", the poet's attention is on the people of India. He is critical of the Doctrine of Maya, one of the pillars of Vedanta, the philosophy and teachings of the *Vedas* and the *Upanishads* as interpreted by Sankaracharya. According to the Doctrine of Maya, the world of the senses is unreal, an 'illusion' only. The ultimate reality is the One, the one and only God, the *Atman*, the *Brahman*. This doctrine had and continues to have strong negative impact on the common man and his condition through the ages. The poet ridicules this doctrine and says 'God's world is Mother's lap to all other beings, but you, old dotard, believe in nothing that is near.'

Chitra (1896) The Multicoloured

> *"Sometimes I think, there is a conflict of two opposite forces in me. One is always calling me to quiescence and fulfillment and the other never allowing me to rest. The restlessness of Europe is always hammering at my calm Indian nature. For that reason there is pain on the one hand and detachment on the other hand. There is poetry and there is philosophy. On the one side is my addiction to work and on the other side is attraction to deep thinking. The result is a sense of despair and resignation."*
>
> — *'Sabuj Patra'*, January 29, 1898. Translated by the author.

"*Sonar Tari*" gave first expression to these opposing forces. In *Chitra* we find the conflict of these two forces gradually taking shape and becoming clearer. In fact, the poems in *Chaitali* and *Kanika* have the play of the two forces. In *Kalpana* and *Naibedya* Rabindranath's poetry seem to have taken a turn but the underlying forces are the same. From this standpoint *Sonar Tari* to *Naibedya* (1894-1901) can be called one phase of Rabindranath's poetry.

There are two poems from *Chitra* in this collection. Both are widely admired as great poems. But they are different and represent the opposing forces. In the first poem, "Farewell to Heaven", the poet's heart is crying for the 'indigent afflicted, tearful, sullied' Mother

Earth. The heaven is in his imagination separate and detached from the Creation. The joys and sorrows of the Earth or the loss of one or many humans do not affect the fare of happiness of the gods. Man cannot be satisfied with a monotonous life of unbroken happiness. He becomes restless for a varied and greater life on earth. Happiness may be short-lived and peace may be rare here but man's fulfillment can only be found on this earth.

> "So let nectar flow in heaven, and love as such
> Ever mixed with pain and pleasure, on earth flowing,
> Keep the earth's heaven-spots evergreen with tears streaming."
>
> — "Farewell to Heaven", p.69.

Earth — she is no heaven, but she is a motherland. Both joy and sorrow are present here and that is her pride. Heaven has happiness but no joy. It can only be found on earth. There is no fulfilment here but only its hint; man does not find the destination but can enjoy the journey. The sorrow and the unfulfillment of life create a struggle that is uniquely human.

The second poem 'Urvashi' (p.75) is unique and glorious in the supreme fulfillment of beauty. Here beauty is painted on the canvas of the universe. Urvashi, you are "not mother, nor daughter, nor a wife". She does not light the evening lamp in any home, nor does she go to the bridal bed with hesitant steps and trembling heart. She is "like a flower without stem" blooming on her own in the primal dawn. This beauty is beyond any human relationship and it is also timeless. The poet is purely romantic here, "From aeons past you're the beloved of all on this earth's face/O Urbashi, of incomparable grace." There is a tinge of tear, sadness in the incomparable beauty. Otherwise it would have been like the heaven – perfect — and could not satisfy us mortals.

Chaitali **(1896),** Chaitra Harvest

The poems in this book were written at the end of one winter and during the summer while the poet was on a boat on a small river in Patisar in East Bengal. The river was no Padma, but was most ordinary, slow moving and not too wide. Like the river, the poems written have no exuberance of emotions, no adorned language and the subjects seem to be snap shots taken from a close distance. They come from contentment, calmness, and maturity. Appropriately, the poems are mostly sonnets. Lyrical poems move in fast rhythm, sonnets do not have that movement. They can be written leisurely and in simple language. The poems of *Chaitali* are of this type.

Great lyrical poets are generally not great sonnet writers, Shelley, Swinburne, and Rabindranath too. Michael Madhusudan wrote great sonnets in Bengali, each built like a great mansion with one marble stone upon another. Rabindranath's sonnets have fourteen lines. That is all the similarity that they have with English sonnets. Unlike Madhusudan, he did not pay attention to the rules of sonnets or their rhyming scheme. He created his own rules. But they are great in their ideas and mood.

The ideas in Rabindranath's poems in his previous books find concrete shape in *Chaitali.* His love for people transforms into love for his country. This love again flows in two direction — one stream flows towards the past and the other stays in the present. The poet's love for people has taken one step forward to embrace the neglected and poor of the society. With another step it extends towards all beings in Nature. One can easily understand that the love poems in *Chaitali* are not written for any God or to any lady of the mind (*Manashi*).

The first sonnet in this collection is critical of Hindu superstition about physical purity of the temple where a ragged poor man can defile the sanctity of the temple. The temple priest knows the scripture but is ignorant about the presence of God in every being as taught in the first verse of the *Isha Upanishad,*" "Know this, all this, whatever moves in this moving world, is enveloped by God." The message of the second sonnet is about his love and reverence for even the insignificant place of the earth and for the life that has the least worth. The third sonnet, "The First Kiss" is noteworthy. It would have been a mundane poem if it were the first kiss of two lovers. But the poet has set it against the background of peals of temple bells and the assembly of the stars in the sky that made the two lovers realise that no one is alone and isolated in this world. All are connected. In the fourth poem, not a sonnet, the poet sings about his closeness with rural Bengal.

Kanika (1899) Particles.

The poems in this book are mostly epigrams, light hearted and witty but very deep in ideas often revealing great wisdom in simple language.

Kshanika (1900) The Flitting One.

Rabindranath's deep ideas in light lyrics are at their best in *Kshanika*. The style is easy going, the language close to spoken language, serious ideas are cloaked in light satire. There is no sign of sadness as in his previous writings. We see the poet in intimate contact with his environment, people, and rural life.

In "Two Shores", p.89, the people on the two shores are secondary here. The primary objects are the sandy beaches of autumn on one shore and the forest on the other shore. Between the two shores flows the river with is many messages. The presence of the two people on the two shores has been captured beautifully as if in a framed picture.

Wit and satire dominate the second poem, "Scriptures Says" (p.93), which is a total rejection of the conservative Hindu idea of retreating into a forest in the third phase of life. Mocking this idea the poet is saying that the forest life is more appropriate for youth, as it is full of beauty and offers opportunities for doing things that young people really like to do. Staying home is more appropriate for the elderly for minding their earthly possessions.

Kalpana (1900) Imagination
Naibedya (1901) Offerings to God

These two books, along with *Katha* (1900) (and not included in this collection) are the history of Rabindranath's mental journey into India's past. It is the beginning of the poet's multi-faceted poetic life. In *Kalpana* he has written about the grandeur of poetry and legends of the past. In *Naibedya* he has written about the lofty ideas and ideals of ancient India. The first twenty-one and the last poems are songs. The remaining seventy-eight are sonnets in Rabindranath's own style.

The main theme of *Naibedya* is the poet's keen interest in the spiritual ideas of ancient India. He tried to understand the spiritual message of bygone days. In the light of that understanding he tried to see the India of his time, the Western ideals and the ideals of humanism. It is important to understand the main messages of the spirituality of ancient India or at least how the poet understood them. In his essay on "*Pracin Bharater Ekah: Dharma*" (The One Ancient India: Dharma) Rabindranath wrote:

> *"Ugliness is in the fragments, beauty is in the One; striving is in fragments, peace is in the One; conflict is in fragments, the good is in the One. Likewise death is in the fragments and immortality is in the One. If I break the One into thousands of pieces and look at them I cannot protect myself from the many. Then material world becomes supreme. Wealth, fame, kith, and kin become paramount and take us on a merry go round, possessions, cars, bricks and mortars become important; we find no end to our pursuit to increase the quantity of our possessions and engage in endless competition with our neighbours."*

—*Rabindra Rachanabali*, Vol. 12, p.32. Translated by the author.

The spirituality of ancient India was based on the unity in the diversity and the fragments of the creation. The ancient sages saw the One in many. The human mind, due to its innate nature, knowingly or unknowingly seeks, sometimes in the straightforward way or in a roundabout way, the supreme joy of unity in diversity. And when he has a glimpse of it he declares:

"Hear ye, hear ye,
O the children of immortality
And the gods in heaven, Him I have known

The Great One beyond darkness who alone
Is effulgent. Knowing and seeing Him, I say.
You can conquer death and there is no other way."

— Poem no. 60, Offering to God, p.103.

As stated earlier, ideas are primary in '*Naibedya*' and three ideas are dominant in these poems. First is love for the country. India reached a glorious height in the Vedic era. Because people of India have forgotten those ideals, the country is now impoverished spiritually, politically, socially, and economically. Secondly, devotion to God, the God whom Rabindranath has not yet experienced personally but the one he has found in the *Upanishads* and in the general environment of the *Brahmo Samaj*. Thirdly, his genuine quest for the good of all humanity.

The poems in *Naibedya* in the collection here fall into the above categories. These poems and the others in *Naibedya* have many memorable messages spiritual advice, but many of them cannot be called real poetry. *Naibedya* is perhaps Rabindranath's weakest poetry book.

Smaran **(1903)**, Remembering

Mrinalini Devi, Rabindranath's wife died of an undiagnosed illness on November 23, 1902. She was barely twenty-nine and Rabindranath was forty-one-and-a half years old. Earlier in his life at age twenty-four the poet suffered the loss of a friend, his sister-in-law. The two deaths merged into one and haunted his poetry and songs with unconsummated longing. Many of his poems and songs would be shadowed by the "unfinished business" of grieving.

The poems in *Smaran* were all written about four months after Mrinalini's death. In this book we see the poems centred on the poet himself, his wife, and his relationship with her. Surprisingly, we find no trace of doubt in his faith in God. Although doubt or questioning is a natural reaction to the death of a loved one, it is almost absent in Rabindranath's poetry. Instead we find that the poet is seeing the loved one in the beauty of the Creation and in all humanity and ultimately in the protection of the almighty. (Poem no. 29, p.99).

Most of the poems in this book can not be called good poetry. Good poetry requires not only real life experience but also the perspective that time can give. The poems in *Smaran* did not have the benefit of passage of time.

Shishu (1903) The Child

Half of the poems in this book were written much earlier, at the beginning of his poetic career. These poems were transferred from other books to *Shishu.* It should also be remembered that the poet lost his mother when he was fourteen. Nine months after Rabindranath's wife's death, his second daughter, Renuka (Rani) died of tuberculosis in 1903. Some of the poems in *Shishu* were written in the Almora Hills when the poet had taken his daughter there for a change of air before her death.

Though the poems can't be called dramatic, they have an element of drama in them. There are three characters in these poems: the child (*shishu*), his mother and his father. The father mostly remains in the background. We mostly hear the voices of the child and his mother and never the voice of the poet. But the voice of the poet comes out clearly in the child's voice. These poems appear to be the poet's fulfillment of his relationship with his lost mother in the world of his imagination. It is amazing to see how mature Rabindranath was able to penetrate children's imaginative minds and describe in their language their many moods and thoughts.

In poem, 'Critic' (p.111) Rabindranath shows the depth of his familiarity with the psychology of a child. The differential treatment of the mother towards the father and the son appears odd to the child's mind. His reasoning becomes credible as those of a child in the poet's words. Going further into the mind of the child we arrive in his fairy-tale land in the poem, *King's Castle* (p.113). No one knows where the king's castle is. It is only known to the child's imagination, on the roof where the potted *tulsi* plant is. In real life there was a potted *tulsi* plant on the roof of Rabindranath's house. The place was full of mystery when the poet was a child himself.

The reference of the barber may seem strange to some readers. In old days barbers used to go from house to house and from village to village for their business. So they heard gossips from their clients. It was something similar to the beauty parlours of modern days. In the child's imagination his secret was safe, for only he and his pet kitten knew where the barber's village was. It was the same secret place where the king's castle was.

Kheya (1906) The Ferry

From 1902 (after *Naibedya)* to 1914 (*Balaka)* the onward movement of Rabindranath's poetry was obstructed and it took a turn in a new direction. This turn will be discussed in the *Gitanjali* phase. During this period, notable poetry books were *Kheya, Shishu*, and *Utsarga.* During this period he wrote many novels, plays, and essays in prose.

It is necessary to know a few facts about Rabindranath's life in this period to understand the poems of *Kheya.* We have noticed that *Naibedya* was the poet's mental journey into ancient India's glorious spiritual and high human values world. *Kheya* was written after his return from this mental journey to the Bengal of that time. Bengal was in ferment and in a bitter political struggle with the British *Raj* to "unsettle the settled" fact of the division of Bengal. Rabindranath jumped into the fray with both feet. He was busy giving lectures and presiding over many protest meetings and editing many magazines at that time. He had dreams that India would be on the road to greatness again through this struggle. Soon he found that there was no trace of the greatness of ancient India in the India of that time. He found no echo of the past in the reality of the day. In his mental exploration of India's past he learnt of her greatness in spiritual ideas and high standard of human values. In the political movement of his day he found pedantic ideas, lack of ideals and low moral and human values. Rabindranath was profoundly disappointed and disheartened and he left the movement and any active role in politics for good. He lost his mental equilibrium, which is essential for writing good poetry.

Kheya was written during this period. The flow of Rabindranath's poetry was always towards mankind. He paid his greatest homage to man and not to God or even to Nature. His disappointment with the political movement obstructed this flow. We see in *Kheya* the dark shadow of sadness, hopelessness and farewell (p.117). The poet was 'neither homebound nor bound for shore', he lost the comfort of home and he did not find shelter on the other shore. But all is not dark. He sees an 'obscure vision's gleam' on the other shore, though he does not know what it is.

Like the poem on p.117 there are other poems with a similar setting and theme in this book and in the three volumes in the *Gitanjali* phase. The time is twilight or dark night and the place is the riverbank or a wide-open space. In such a time and place ordinary people tend to think about the mystery of life and Nature and along with comes a detached mood. It is natural that a poet like Rabindranath would be self-absorbed.

The poems in *Kheya* became difficult for people to understand. Critics accused him of being a 'mystic', a copycat of western poetry, and so on. But every one agreed of one thing, that Rabindranath had lost his poetic genius. No one really understood him.

Gitanjali (**1910**) Song Offering
Gitimalya (**1914**) Garland of Songs
Gitali (**1914**) Harvest of Songs

A number of devastating incidents in Rabindranath's public and personal life affected him so gravely that the main flow of his poetry came to a halt for over twelve years. In the public arena the chasm between the ideals of India of the Vedic period and the reality of India of his time shocked and disappointed him and made him withdrawn. In his personal life, the loss of one loved one after another affected him gravely. We have seen the poet's grief of the death of his wife in 1902 in *Smaran*. Within nine months the poet lost his second daughter, Rani, in 1903. The poet's younger son, Shamindranath (Shami) fell a victim to cholera while holidaying in Bihar in 1907. The poet was also suffering from ill health during this period.

One death after another, and his own weak health turned Rabindranath's thoughts from the outside world and humanity to the world within. His thoughts and his poetry became steeped in devotion to his Lord, friend and beloved. The influence of the teachings of the *Upanishads* and his father was always an important element in his mental makeup and poetry from the beginning. But it was not the primary aspect of this poetry. The poet's devotion to God, which was a bud for so long, blossomed as a hundred-petal lotus in the three volumes of songs. *Gitanjali, Gitimalya, and Gitali.* The lyrical poems (songs) of this period gave him the greatest honour of the literary world, the Nobel Prize in 1913, and propelled him on the world scene as a great poet and philosopher. The great lyrical poems in these three books are only a branch of his life-long works. The songs in *Gitimalya* are more beautiful than those in *Gitanjali.* In *Gitali* they seem to have lost their momentum.

It is in *Gitanjali* that we find for the first time songs purely about love of Nature. Before this phase, Nature came into his poetry following man. Here Nature is in her own glory. Later Nature would be more firmly established and expressed more clearly in his many songs. The difference between love for a person and love for Nature is that human love has conflict and love for Nature has not. She does not assert and she has no expectations. We can love her in our own way without any conflict and any obstruction.

Rabindranath's relationship with God in this phase is a bit different from that of a devoted saint. A saint is happy to give his all to his God without wanting anything in return. He loses himself in God. But the poet of *Gitanjali* does not lose himself in God. He not only gives his all but also wants in return. This 'wanting' comes from love and not from devotion. He gives to his Lord but wants from his beloved. We see both self-surrender and self-expression working simultaneously.

An exceptional feature of many songs in the three books is the way Rabindranath accepted sorrow and misfortune. To him, God came down to his devotee mystically through trials and tribulations. Another kind of sorrow we find in *Gitanjali*, time and again. It is the pain of separation from his beloved and the pain of not getting Him intimately. Rabindranath thought about the suffering and sorrow of all humanity in *Naibedya* (at the beginning of the *Gitanjali* phase). He would think about it in *Balaka* at the end of the *Gitanjali* phase.

In this phase, the pain and sorrow are his personally. The voice speaking to us in *Gitanjali* is his own. It comes from his personal experience and feelings and he expressed them in lyrics that touched all sensitive hearts all over the world.

The songs in this collection are all from my previous books, *Songs of Rabindranath Tagore,* published by Shipra Publications, New Delhi. The themes discussed here can be found in the poems included in this collection.

Utsarga (1914) Dedications

There is little history behind this book. In 1903-4 Mohit Chandra Sen published an anthology of Rabindranath's poetry up to that time. He divided the book into nine chapters according to theme. The poet wrote introductions to these chapters. This book mostly contains the poems written as an introduction to the chapters of this anthology. The prominent notes are longing and unattained quest. His quest was to know the life of ordinary people. He tried to enter into people's lives sometimes through the front gate of the present, sometimes crossing the moat of the past and other times from the sky and through his love for God. He only reached the gate but could not enter, so he has to be content playing his flute sitting by the gate. The melody is of longing, disappointment, and resignation. The two poems in this collection reflect these themes.

We will find later the poet on his deathbed saying "I could only enter the courtyard of the common people's home but not into their living quarters." In spite of this admitted failure to know the common man intimately his faith in humanity and its goodness and his sense of unity with all humanity never failed him. We will see it clearly in his last poem, a testament to his unwavering faith.

The *Balaka* Phase

Included in this phase are Rabindranath's poetry books published between 1916 to 1929.

Balaka (1916) Wild Geese

The poems in *Balaka* were written in 1914 and 1915. He began to write them shortly after he came back to India, completing seventeen months travel in Europe and America. During his travels he came in close contact with the people and their lives in these countries. The experience brought the onward flow of his poetry back to its original course, towards mankind and his sense of unity with humanity.

Rabindranath turned his face from the outside world to the world within, in the *Gitanjali* phase. In *Balaka*, the poet emerged as a poet of the world with more fervour than ever before. The pace of life in Europe and America seemed to him like a wide and fast flowing river with its big waves moving in a way that he had never seen in India. The flow of the river of life in India seemed to be dead. Life in India was limited in its scope and sphere of action and influence compared to the vast expanse of life and activity in Europe and America. They were vibrant and not stagnant. These countries were moving forward and not paralysed by the overwhelming power of ghosts of the past. The mankind he was searching for so long, found only a fraction in India, he found it fully expressed in the vast arena of Europe and America. This experience had profound impact on this poetry in *Balaka* and continued till the end of his life.

Rabindranath's poetry turned towards mankind in *Balaka* but its form and sound were no longer the same as before. The experience of the *Gitanjali* phase retained its impression on the poet and made his poetry more varied, colourful, and complex. His reasons for introspection and self-concern were gradually disappearing. Grief was removed from his heart and was now present only in his imagination. The poet regained his lost health and his life found new vitality.

In *Sandhyasangit,* Rabindranath emerged from the influence of the form and language of his predecessors. His language was modern, close to the Bengali spoken language, the movement (rhythm) of his poetry was fast and the sound was lyrical. He gained another characteristic of his artistry in *Manashi* and *Sonar Tari,* firmness or strength in his language, reflecting control over his emotion. In *Gitanjali* phase, rhythm became predominant because the poems were songs. The interrelation and conflict of movement and firmness of language dominated Rabindranath's poetry from *Sonar Tari* to *Naibedya.* In *Kalpana* we saw firmness of language coming out as the dominant force.

In *Balaka,* the poet found a 'new frame' for his poetry to shape his new found vitality and his new experience abroad. Here we find the subject matter or the mood and subject controlling the structure of each stanza. Of the forty-five poems in *Balaka,* the first thirty-four were written in 1914 and the remaining eleven in 1915. Each stanza in ten of these poems has the same structure and length and one is a sonnet. Each stanza has different structure and length in the balance thirty-four poems. Though written in the couplet form, the lengths of lines (and syllables) are also unequal in these poems. The style of these thirty-four poems is known as '*Mukta Chanda*' or '*Balaka rhyme*' in Bengali poetry.

The First World War began at the time of writing these poems though the war drums had sounded earlier. The poet could hear 'the thunder of death'. The pain and suffering of the world overwhelmed him. They also prompted him to action. Never before we have seen Rabindranath so conscious of the perils and evil facing humanity and so concerned about the prospect. He decided that he must call people to come out of their self-centred world into the arena of all humanity for the good of all.

The impact of the war on the poet can be seen clearly in poem 37 of *Balaka* (p.145). It was written in 1915 and is one of his great poems. The monstrosity of the war had a new awakening in the consciousness of the "indifferent" poet. Questions arose in his mind about justice in the world and about the fairness of the justice of the omnipotent and the omniscient. He realised that "drained was the capital of the truth of the past" and the "stagnant time in the port" of *Gitanjali* must come to an end. The poet has heard the "din of wailing" and "the clamour of blood from a million hearts gushing"

"The current of rage surging,
Clouds of poisoned breath swelling
Make the heaven and earth faint, bewilder

And clasp one death after another,
Surmounting all, a way must be found
For the boat to be onward bound
For a new ocean shore, — "

But Rabindranath did not know at that time the "new ocean shore" or how it would look. He only knew

"Unknown is the seashore, unknown is the land,
For that place
From the empty space
Sounds a fierce call in the roaring gale."

In stanza after stanza we hear a distressed and anxious refrain, "Stagnant time in the port must end here." The war was mainly a European war. But soldiers from India were also among the casualties. The poet was grieved by its horror, wherever it happened. The war was causing untold misery in so many lands. So many parents were losing their children, so many wives were losing their husbands and so many innocent people were suffering and losing their lives. For whose sin was the world now facing this calamity?

Rabindranath gave the answer in a lecture in Shantiniketan at that time. "The punishment does not come from where the evil is. Why is the impact of the pain and suffering throughout the world? But remember this, there no discontinuity in humanity, all mankind is one. For this reason the burden of evil deeds of the father has to be borne by the son, a friend has to atone for a friend's sin and the weak must suffer the persecution and oppression of the powerful." This may be a sound statement of fact but it can't be called justice. So the poet says that it is useless to search for the evildoer; all of us bear the responsibility for this calamity. So

"Single mindedly press on,
Cross this ocean of destruction
To a new beginning nigh
Holding the new victory banner high"

I said earlier that the poet has no new hypothesis or no solution to end all wars. It is for this reason the poem is so credible. He took the high road of stating the truth rather than suggesting a solution. The poet is not afraid but he has high hopes that there would be an end to the calamity and the "gate of a new golden dawn will open at the end of the dark night." Otherwise,

"The cost of braves' blood, mothers' tears rain
Will they be lost in the dusts of the earth in vain?
Will not paradise be won?
Will not payment for all the debts be done
By the keeper of the world's treasure?
Will not the quest through the night usher
A new dawn?
In the night of untold affliction,
At death's invitation,
When man shattered his mortal limit
Would not then be seen the infinite glory's summit?"

The poem ends with questions. We may assume that the answer is certainly "yes." But it is conditional. Man can see the "infinite glory's summit" only if he shatters his mortal limit of ignorance, hatred and conflict. Maybe the poet is saying that God's immortal glory is not yet manifested and it will not be until mankind can evolve to the highest height and reach godhead. The poet then declares that God is nothing but the full expression of humanity in love, peace, and truth — "Peace is truth, auspicious is truth, truth is one and timeless."

The contradiction between the poet's love for the living in this world and the sure knowledge that he must leave this world is the subject of poem number 19 of *Balaka* in this collection (p.141). In his songs we have seen the poet inviting death as "sweet lord" and "beloved" and "ultimate fulfillment of life". But here death to him is opposed to life. Rabindranath explained this paradox in prose.

"I want the world so dearly and I must leave it too. If these two are equally true and yet contradictory then the burden of this conundrum would be on this world and it would have been a deceit. Then I

would have seen signs of crookedness in the world's beauty. But I see that nowhere. Then where is the unity of these two truths? The answer can't be found in poetry."

— Translation by the author.

When poetry ends in reasoning it may indicate a flaw in the poet's realisation. In spite of it the poem is not a mediocre one, because there is a secondary meaning transcending the primary meaning of the poet's words in this poem. The poet's distress at this apparent contradiction and his anxious longing for a unity make this poem enjoyable.

"Amidst these two there is somewhere unity.
    Or this universe with certainty
Could not bear with smile
    For so long this splendid beguile."

The poem number 28 in *Balaka* is about another experience of the poet, presented very skilfully. Why did God create this vast universe of life if He were complete and fulfilled? Does He have any wants? Or does He want to enjoy his creation by making man and only through man's joy and sorrow, wants and complaints and above all man's love, to enjoy his own creation? Man appears to be his mirror to observe His fulfillment and his unending splendour and treasure.

Palataka (1918) The Runaway

The poet had created a new style in rhymed Bengali poetry in *Balaka* where the length of the stanzas in a poem is different and so is the length of lines. The language was bold and adorned, with the choice of words and their arrangements expressing the poet's passion and emotion and the subject was mainly the issues and problems facing humanity.

In *Palataka* the same style of poetry is there but in a new form. The form is unadorned. Everyday words are arranged in simple fashion, easy flowing, clear and free. All the poems in this book were written in 1918. We find the poet moved by the pain and pleasure and incidents of everyday life. The poems in many cases are stories. Storytelling seems to be more important than poetry. We see poetry in sudden flashes of similes and metaphors here and there, in the hints of images and scattered sentences with deep meaning.

For example, in "The Runaway" (p.155) a pet deer and a puppy were playing in the poet's garden when

"In Phalgun comes the fitful south wind, the sky felt a tremor
of receiving a love letter from a lover.
Flower–fest began in the *shal* tree stand
Gentle throb ran through the leaves and the grassland.
We had no inference
When the deer got, from whom, the message of indifference."

Then

"On one afternoon bright
When the *amlaki* stand was excited at the play of shimmering
light,
The warm air was heavy with mango blossoms' scent
Life or death became one on their own
And he had no fear of the unknown."

The poet's uncommon gifts of describing the beauty of Nature and creating a mysterious feeling about life in only a few superbly crafted lines are apparent here. Only in a few poems in *Palataka* does the poet deal with social problems like the sad plight of women in Indian joint family system or in the lives of widows. Otherwise most of the poems in this book deal with the human mind. In the "Last Foundation," (p.159) we see either the death or impending death of the poet's eldest daughter Bela casting a pall over this poem. Bela died of tuberculosis after prolonged suffering (like his other daughter Renuka some fifteen years earlier) in 1918, the year of publication of *Palataka.*

Shishu Bholanath (1923) The Child Bholanath

In this book we find the poet again exploring the mind of a child. The comments made earlier about *Shishu* are all applicable here. But the child here is more imaginative and his thoughts are more deep and mysterious. The poet seems to be looking into the mind of a child from a distance with great sympathy and he is enjoying the play of the young person.

Purabi (1925) Musical Raga for the Evening
Mahua (1929) The Indian Butter Tree

Most of the poems in *Purabi* were written during the poet's travels in South America in 1924. We see the shadow of pain and sorrow in this. The poet is not mortified. He is rather serene and peaceful like the sweet and beautiful picture he has painted of the approaching of sunset in the ocean. The poet is an observer of this beauty but he is sad that the darkness of night would soon wipe it out. No matter how much he tries a poet can't capture it in words.

Purabi is the name of an evening raga in Indian classical music. Its tune is sad, because the day is over. The poet was in his sixties, his twilight years, at the time of writing *Purabi*. "The Image" describes twilight hour of the day, a sad but beautiful metaphor for life, which may well be wiped out soon by death, a metaphor for darkness of night. This sadness is the tune of *Purabi*.

There is a little history about *Mahua*. A few of his friends wanted an anthology of the poet's love poems to be published. The idea was that such a book would be appropriate as a wedding gift. They asked the poet to write a few love poems to go with the old ones and the poet obliged. He wrote many love poems for the book and they are his best poems of love. But not all of them are about the joy of union of two persons; they are about separation and farewell of lovers too. It is the case with the short poem in this collection (p.173). The poet has explained the reason himself:

> "* * * *Made to the order is like the starter of a car. It only starts the car and then the car runs by its own mechanical mechanism. It*

*forgets about the push. The poems in Mahua also undoubtedly forgot their first push completely at the time of writing the poems. The innate nature of electrical current of imagination from its eternal inspiration moved the poems. * * *"*

—From a letter of the poet published as introduction to *Mahua*. Translation is by the author.

The Last Phase (1932-41)

The last ten years of Rabindranath's life as a poet are amazing for more than one reason. The most amazing features of this period are the volume of works, novelty of presentation, bold and unhindered expression. The sheer volume of songs and poems in the last ten-year period surpasses the quantity of output in any other decade of his life of eighty years. He wrote more than twenty volumes of songs and poems during this period. I have included poems from twelve of these books in this collection. It is incredible to see no hint or sign of old age in any of these poems. Their brilliance is untarnished and their variety is endless. Their beauty and treasure of imagination, vision and vast variety dazzle us up to his last book, *Shesh Lekha* (Last Writings). It is true that during the last two years the flow was gradually diminishing, as was his life force. But the poetry did not lose their meaning, expression and depth. They were as fresh as ever, constantly showing new outlook and innovation.

Parisesh (The End) and *Punsacha* (Postscript) were published within one month in 1932. The name, The End, suggests perhaps that Rabindranath thought it to be his last poetry book. He did not know at that time that some of his best poems were yet to be written. The two books are quite different in their theme and poetic style. On the one hand we find his 'doubts', 'questions' and the play of the opposite forces in his mind and his deep disappointment and on the other hand the terrible side of the world in his poetry and his humanism stronger than ever. Also we find his innovative style of prose poetry for the first time in *Punascha*. There was a hint of an unknown 'new sea shore' and a 'new land' in poem number 37 of *Balaka*. We see that land in these two books for the first time.

Rabindranath wrote prose poetry in "*Lipika*" in 1892. He did not have the "courage" to publish it as prose poetry and the book was published as prose. But many readers read it as poetry because of its lyrical style. Rabindranath is the father of prose poetry in Bengali literature and four books, *Punascha* (Postscript), *Shesh Saptak* (The Last Octave), *Patraput* (Plate Made from Leaves) and *Shyamali* (She Who is Dark) are perfect examples of this style. They are not free verses without end rhymes but prose with its own rhythm.

The poet's pen is not tired in *Rogashajyay* (On the Sickbed), *Arogya* (Recovery) or even in *Sesh Lekha* (Last Writings). The physical pain and mental agony are there but there is no sign of old age or infirmity anywhere in his mind. The very best kind of poetry expresses apparently quite contradictory feelings or tension as in "The Ode to Nightingale" by Keats or in "The Four Quarters" by Eliot. Evil and bliss are the two sides of the same coin, said Rilke. In *Prantik* (The Borderland) Rabindranath lamented (in number 10) that his life was coming to its end and yet he did not get recognition as a poet of the terrible for "The sublime image of the terrible did not appear" in his heart. That is true. The poet's yearning for the presence of the evil in his poetry and genuine pain or its absence are the crowning success of his poetry of the last ten years.

The evil appeared in his poetry in *Balaka* in the bright light of the reality of the First World War. But the poet was not mentally equipped to accept it. Nor did he accept it in *Naibedya*. In both cases Rabindranath took the worldwide suffering of humanity as God's punishment for man's evil deed.

Parisesh (1932) The End

The poem, "The Question", in *Parisesh* is widely known and acclaimed. Historically, the poem was written immediately after the failure of the Round Table Conference in London and the imprisonment of Mahatma Gandhi by the *Raj*. Some people have attributed this poem as the poet's protest of this event. Personally I do not agree with this view. I believe Rabindranath's protest had a broader context. It was against the brutality of the *Raj* in general and cruel treatment of the prisoners in Buxar fort and the killing of two political prisoners there by the British at that time.

Coming back to the poem, "The Question", (p.175) we can say that in this "pitiless world" many barbaric acts happen that can not be forgiven. For example, September 11, 2001 terrorist attacks on the US. There are some sinners in this world that we cannot love. Yet

> "My lord", Your many prophets, saints and sages.
> "Love all, forgive, and rid your hearts of the venom
> Of violence," they told through the ages."

The poet turned them back from the courtyard with only a "vain salutation." In the last four lines in utter agony the poet asks,

> "Have You forgiven and loved,"/I ask my Lord, as I shed a tear,
> "Those who snuffed Your light/and poisoned Your atmosphere?"

The unwritten question is, "Why did your saints and sages give this inappropriate or even unjust advice?" This poem and others in *Parisesh* point us to the new land of *Balaka*.

Rabindranath wrote frequently about pain and suffering. Never before had he written about the suffering that has no end and no remedy. Although he had contact with people, he had not seen or his poetry never reflected the brutality by man on a world scale before. We see that stated clearly and unequivocally in *Parisesh* in this poem and more so in other poems of the book.

Punascha (Postscript)
Shesh Saptak (The Last Octave)
Patraput (Plate Made of Leaves)
Shyamali (She Who is Dark)

Punascha (1932), (Postscript)

It is the first of the four poetry books that Rabindranath wrote in prose poetry. It has not only a new poetic style but also the subject matter, language and expression are all new. The kind of songs and poems the poet had written for so long were not centred on ordinary man nor did they express his feelings. Their language and expression were also removed from those of ordinary folks. The poet decided to write about things familiar to ordinary people and in their style. So we find the poems in this phase familiar images painted in primary colours; the language is simple and easy going and free from the tyranny of conventional rules of poetry.

Some of the poems in the *Punascha* are stories, such as "The Guilty" and "Camellia" in this collection. "Camellia" is about unrequited love but the poet is more interested in telling the story than about the feelings of the characters. The poet is missing the absence of someone close to him in "Writing A Letter". He does not describe his feelings but they come out vividly in a few words: "There is only one news item — You have left." These three poems have no deeper meaning. They are ordinary stories told in ordinary language. The two poems, "Observation" and "Beautiful", describe two different days in the rainy season. Like flashes of lighting, beautiful smiles dazzle our eyes. The poet is conscious of his seventy years of age but his mind goes into the past to some rainy days, perhaps on the Padma, and he wants to keep the memory of these days "woven as a tapestry with the rhymes" of his idleness.

The poem, "The Flute" (p.199) is a much-loved one. The metaphors, the similes and the imagery are superbly sculptured. The poem is written in first person singular. The poet speaks as a poorly paid clerk in a merchant's office and his poverty is so abject that a lizard fares better than he does.

> "Along with me there is another creature
> in my room. His rent is included in mine:
> he is a lizard.
> The difference between him and me is this:
> he has no want of food."

A few short lines speak volumes. He spends the evening in the clamour of the railway station to save the cost of electricity and then returns to the "loneliness, absolute silence and darkness" of his room. During the day "the dark shadow of the rain clouds" in his room "is in a lifeless swoon like an animal caught in a snare." The clerk finds himself "fastened fast to some half dead world."

"In the nooks and crannies of the alley —
mango peels and stones, discards of jack-fruit,
gills of fish,
a dead kitten maybe and
much more trash gather and rot."

I am not sure if Rabindranath ever came into contact with anyone like the luckless "Haripada clerk" in this poem or saw any neighbourhood like the "Kinu milkman's alley". But his description of the life and living condition of Haripada is so vivid, intimate and real that they make the poem believable and beautifully sad. The agony of the loveless life of the clerk is described poignantly in just four lines:

"She didn't come to my home,
but she comes to my mind all the time —
wearing a *Dhaka-sari* and a vermilion
dot adorning her forehead."

When the melody of the flute fills "foul air of the alley" and the sky "with the eternal pain of lovers-apart" the alley becomes "utterly unreal and intolerable as the delirium of a drunk." The clerk finds solace in the world of his imagination:

"This tune is real
where in an endless
twilight hour
flows the Dhaleswari.
On her bank is the deep shadow of the dark trees,
In the courtyard awaits for me the one
wearing a *Dhaka-sari* and a vermilion dot on her forehead."

It is this contrast in mood that makes the poem so enjoyable.

The poem, The Flute Player (p.235), in *Shyamali,* is the expression of the suppressed pain and agony in the woman's heart in a male dominated society. The Flute Player is the allegorical hero who plays the tune of emancipation. We don't know if the Flute Player is a man or a woman, perhaps a woman who can take the 'woman' to the dreamland where she would have a fulfilled life. Rabindranath could feel the agony in the woman's heart and the poem is an artistic and skilful presentation of that feeling.

To understand the life and mind of Rabindranath one has to carefully read his poetical works from *Shesh Saptak* and *Patraput* to his last book, *Sesh Lekha*. Having come to the end of his life the poet is busy in finding the essence of his life and it's experience. His analysis is from many angles — spiritual, intellectual and historical. His sight is penetrating and his self-analysis and understanding of himself are always stated clearly and boldly and with humility. Much "unfinished business" and dissatisfaction with what he could not achieve caused deep pain in the poet in this period.

We find the poet seeking solace in the beauty of nature. Whenever the suffering and pain in his personal life or in the life of humanity we find him time and again immersed in the tranquillity and beauty of nature. This is most prominent in the poems of *Shesh Saptak*, *Patraput* and *Shyamali* in this collection.

The poem number 3 from *Patraput* (p.227) in this collection is exceptional and majestic. In fact most of the poems in this book are different from the other three books written in prose poetry. The poems are largely about the normal world. Their theme is not the beauty of Nature but the processes that govern Nature. We have not seen the poet articulating the natural processes since *Balaka*. The language is more close to Sanskrit and has little resemblance to spoken Bengali. The poet had combined Sanskritic diction with metreless verse technique. Rabindranath invented the prose poetry technique primarily for more domestic subject matter. He chose Sanskrit language and diction here to create the sound and form appropriate for the theme of this poem.

Beauty, unity and harmony in nature dominated Rabindranath's world of Nature. But in this poem the unity and harmony in Nature appear in a harsh and inhuman form. The poem begins with a series of opposites in Creation such as "sweetness and harshness", "male and female" — attraction and repulsion, centripetal and centrifugal force and "intolerable conflict" between opposite forces. This conflict or *dvandva* is the main theme of this poem.

From the second to the fifth stanza the poet has described the scientific view of the Earth, which is characterised as uncaring and aloof. Though the poet has used mythological symbolism the impression of Darwin in unmistakable. Rabindranath had knowledge of many branches of science including Physics, Astrophysics, Astronomy and Biology. And he knew Darwin's Theory of Evolution very well. It is also equally possible that the inspiration came from the *Vedas*, which he knew only too well. The Vedic view of Creation is the same as the Big Bang theory of Creation of modern cosmology. Fire was the first manifestation of the unmanifested *Brahman*, the ultimate reality. In the *Vedas*[1] the centrifugal force at the moment of creation is described as *Utkranti* and the opposite centripetal force as *Adana* and the balance of the two created motion (and hence matter). The name of the balance or equilibrium was called *Pratistha*. Later these three forces were personified as *Rudra*, *Vishnu* and *Brahma* — the trinity of the Hindu pantheon. Since the Creation is the result of opposite forces we see duality everywhere, heat and cold, light and darkness, construction and destruction, motion and rest, love and hate, joy and sorrow and so on. The Creation is a balance of conflict, power and not a serene harmony. This is the harsh Reality of Nature. The end of the poem leads us deep into that Reality, as Rabindranath understood it. Finally the poet says:

> "O indifferent Earth,
> before I am utterly forgotten
> let me offer at your ruthless feet
> my salutation."

It must be noted that Rabindranath is calling the Earth indifferent, *udasin*, and not God, because the poet's God is not indifferent. He is kind and very much involved with His Creation.

---

1. Hindu Polytheism by Alain Danielou, Published by Bollingen Foundation, N.Y. 1964, p. 22.

Bichitritita (1932) She Who is Many Coloured

There were thirty-one prints of paintings and sketches by Rabindranath, Gaganendranath, Abanindranath, Nandalal and a few other contemporary artists of Bengal in this book. Needless to say, Gaganendranath, Abanindranath and Nandalal were the most famous and talented artists of their time. Rabindranath wrote a poem for each of the painting or sketch. But these poems do not show the genius of Rabindranath, the poet. They do not excel in their imaginative artistry or demonstrate any new insight.

Prantik (1938) The Borderland

Rabindranath fell ill all of a sudden on September 10, 1937 and he was unconscious for two days. The poems in this book are about the poet's experience in the borderland between life and death. They were written during his convalescence period. The poems are compact and controlled, set in unrhymed lines of equal length. We see the poet slipping into a stupor or coming out of it and seeing his life and his world with a new insight. In poem 8 of this book (p.156) the poet thinks that the make–up he had for his stage role is meaningless in the spotlight of his new awakening. He has doubts about the lasting value of his works. We would see it coming again later. Why this doubt? I venture to repeat that his sense of incompleteness comes from his dissatisfaction he felt that his poetry had not captured the 'terribleness' of the world as clearly and forcefully as they should have.

The poem 18 shows his horror and concern of the death and destruction that the impending World War would bring to humanity. The war drums were beating loud. He was calling all to "wage war against the evil beings."

Nabajatak (1940) The Newly Born

In the short introduction to this book Rabindranath wrote, "There have been changes of seasons in my poetry time and again." The name of the book signifies a change of season of his poetry in this book. We find his poetry blossoming in the perfection of historical perspective of the new season. The poet saw life and the world in historical perspective.

In the poem, "Hindustan" (p.249) the poet sees India in the context of her past history. We can see that his understanding is not merely intellectual, it has taken its root deep within the poet's heart and with his new insight he sees "more shadows of ages of decay gathering in the horizon." He gained this insight from the many repetitions of history in India's

" * * * western gate
Where through the ages India's fate
Had always danced in the ground of cremation,
In Delhi, Agra the dance of destruction
With anklets' jingling.

* * *

Where the oppressor and the oppressed made a place
In black and white for playing chess
Today at last
Lies from one end to the other a vast
Graveyard. * * * "

The poet's ominous prediction proved to be true for the people of India for the rulers of India, following historical pattern of ages, "with their glow of riches" would continue and still continues to ignore "the night's darkness" around them.

Rogashajyay (1940) On the Sick-bed
Arogya (1941) Recovery
Janmadine (1941) On My Birthday
Sesh Lekha (1941) Last Writings

These four books were written within a few months time before the poet's death. Rabindranath's last illness started on September 26, 1940. The poems of *Rogashajyay* and *Arogya* were composed by the poet and dictated to others. He was too weak to write himself. He edited them later. These two books have a common thread running through them and will be discussed together.

Generally people's mind become weak from the suffering and pain of terminal illness. They lose faith in the peace and underlying strength of the Creation. They become overwhelmed by personal pain and suffering. It is amazing to see no sign of any such weakness in these poems — either in theme or in presentation.

The poems of the poet's last four books are nearly all unrhymed and free in rhythm. The artistry is simple and the language is unadorned, austere and at times conversational. The subjects are varied and expression is insightful. The poet speaks from his heart about life, people and the everyday world around them. This is his last look at mankind and Nature before his "eyesight is taken back" by the One who had loaned it to him. Nothing escapes from his last look — humanity and Nature, past and present, man working in the fields and factories, the thunder of war and the silence of inner peace, clamour of people and silence of the cosmos, old trees and young corn fields, life and death, grinding of the grindstone by Bhajia and people crossing the river by ferryboat; — all are there. Facing death, the poet is looking at little incidents of life and sights of the world with gratitude and detached love.

In the sombre expression of the poems in *Rogashajyay* we hear the footsteps of imminent death very clearly. We find the poet's mind at peace and his heart at rest in serenity from a deeper understanding of death and suffering. The poet's voice is clear, his expression unadorned, firm and controlled, and his insight is sharp as ever. The subject matter of the poems takes precedence over form and sound.

In poem 10 of *Arogya* the poet returns from thoughts of death to life and from small incidents and scenes to the past history of India and to her present. The empires of the Mughals and other invaders have crumbled, their war drums are silent, "victory monuments, like fools", have forgotten their intent.

> "With bloodied weapons in hand and blood shot looks
> All victors hide their faces in the stories of children's books."

Then

> "Again on those empty roads
> Have come in hordes

On iron paths, riding
Chariots, fire breathing
The mighty English race,
To declare their prowess."

Rabindranath knew from historical precedents that the English too would meet the same fate. It happened only six years later.

Rabindranath now looks at the "earth of clay" and sees "the vast humanity going every day through the ages" to different places, to the fields and factories, to meet life's daily needs. Rabindranath pays his last tribute to the working people who maintain the continuity of flow of history by working with their hands in their homeland and in other lands. Empires after empire crumble but the wheel of work of ordinary man turns forever. Pride of power and might, blood shot eyes of oppressor vanish but the flower, song, love, light of the sun, the autumn morning, the twilight, the morning dewdrop remain. This is the main message of Rabindranath's poetry and the rest are not on his mind when he is about to leave this world.

Rabindranath spent the last days of this life holding fast to the "earth of clay" and "man of clay" in half detached love. In poem 10 of *Janmadine* (p.259) the poet boldly declares, " I'm a poet of the earth" and then answers his critics at home who labelled his poetry mellow, sweet and lacking muscle. The same critics labelled him as a romantic poet, far removed from the ordinary people and their life. The communists in India called him a "reactionary and bourgeois poet." With humility he admits:

"When anywhere rises a sound
In the tune of my flute at once it should resound.
There are many lacunas in my striving
As many calls were not in my hearing.
** **
I don't find the entrance door everywhere.
My station in life stands as the barrier.
The field, the farmer is ploughing;
The fisherman is casting his net, the weaver is weaving —

Their diverse work spreads far and wide
On them, functioning of the whole world resides.
In a tiny corner, in the ever isolation of fame
In society's crest, seated at a narrow window I remain.
Sometimes I have been to the courtyard of the other side
But never had the courage at all to venture inside."

I may be obliged to accept the poet's confession that his poetry has followed many paths but has not gone everywhere. I am not obliged to agree with it wholeheartedly. My reading of his poems, especially those from the *Balaka* period up to his last poem leaves me with the opposite impression. I think the poet was being humble in the above confession and charitable to his critics at the same time. My request to those who share the detractors' sentiment is "Please, do read Rabindranath's poems again and if that won't change your views read them again." The tunes of the poet's flute may be incomplete and one lifetime is never enough for anyone to accomplish all that one wants to do. So Rabindranath leaves the task for completion of his mission to the poet who would be "close to the land." He would eagerly wait to hear that poet's message, which would give voice to "the afflicted, voiceless, silent and standing before the world head bent." The poet also sounds a word of caution to the poet who would be "close to the land." Such a poet must connect his soul with that of the "voiceless" and the "nameless". He/She must command true unity of words and deeds, his/her passion must be genuine and not a "fashion" otherwise the flute's tune will not only be incomplete but a cheap imitation and fool none.

The poet's last book, *Sesh Lekha*, was published after his death with a foreword written by his son, Rathindranath. Poem 15 of this book is the poet's last poem, dictated on July 30, 1941 shortly before being taken to the operating table. He did not recover and passed away eight days later on August 7. The poet did not have the opportunity to edit or correct the poem and it was published as dictated.

In his last testament in poem 15 (p.265) of *Sesh Lekha,* however incomplete it may be, the poet calls Nature an *enchantress.* There is a superficial contradiction in the first fourteen lines of the poem. Nature is depicted as an "enchantress" and at the same time, a "pathfinder." The contradiction is only superficial and not substantial. We can be deceived easily by the splendour of Nature and lulled to think that beauty and harmony is inherent in Nature and there is no real terribleness in this creation. But when we look at the cosmic world we see its terrible side and free ourselves from the many deceptions strewn in the path of creation. The world of the stars is the world of fire and destruction and there is death for mighty stars too. The cosmic world is not pretty but it is sublime.

Rabindranath ends the poem by paying his last respect and homage not to God or even to Nature, but to man. "However crafty outside, he is simple inside. In his heart he receives the truth bathed in his inner-light and nothing can deceive him." Whoever can suffer Nature's trickery receives "everlasting claim to peace." It leaves me with no doubt that the poet received his just reward, his claim to everlasting peace, by suffering calmly and serenely the tricks and treats of Nature's Laws all his life.

About the Book

This collection has 'samples' of poems from most but not from *all* of Rabindranath's poetry publications. The poems included in this book were not selected to illustrate any specific aspect of his poetical genius. Rather, they demonstrate variety of subjects, forms and sounds. The above discussion summarises the messages that I got from this assorted selection.

Rabindranath's poetry was an integral part of the life of all Bengalis of my generation as it was for the lives of two previous generations. Now he is virtually forgotten in the West, remembered outside Bengal as India's Nobel Prize winning poet and even in Bengal he is remembered for the wrong reason, for his songs. There are many reasons for it. Prof. Sisir Kumar Das has discussed some of the reasons in the introductions of the three volumes of *The English Writings of Rabindranath Tagore*, published by the Sahitya Akademy of India. While all may not agree on why or how it happened I think there is unanimity about the fact that not much of his poetry has yet been translated, (disregarding for the moment the quality of translation.)

Translations of poems of the two Persian poets Rumi (1207-73) and Hafiz (1320-89) are readily available in the mainstream bookstores in North America and UK. Translations of Kalidas are also available but not of Rabindranath. I mention these three names for some specific reasons. There are many translations of Rumi and Hafiz who are known as 'Sufi mystics'. While scholars and critics are not completely satisfied with any of the translations, the reading public obviously loves them. The volume of sales proves it. I have mentioned at the beginning that Kalidas and Rabindranath are close to the western mind and surprisingly divergent from the main flow of Indian literature. Yet Kalidas is readily available and not Rabindranath. As a frequent visitor to bookstores this fact intrigued me for a long time. The only rational conclusion I could make was 0accessibility. Rabindranath poetry is available only in Bengali. English translations are rare. The world has forgotten him because Rabindranath was not presented to the world after the excitement over Nobel Prize was over. The Institution which had the copyright never made any effort or encouraged anyone to translate Rabindranath.

This is the reason why I undertook the project. I am well aware of the difficulty of translating poetry from one language to another. Translation of Rabindranath's poetry into English is a daunting task. Any translator of Rabindranath will have to know English and Bengali equally well so as to understand him fully and put him across properly. Though the Bengali language he wrote is simple it is not so easy to understand the meaning. It requires a thorough knowledge and understanding of the *Upanishads*, at least the main concepts in them, because many of his poems are grounded in the philosophy of the *Upanishads*. No one has ever become a great poet without being a great philosopher. And Rabindranath was a poet of poets. These two conditions are very difficult to fulfill. Next, Bengali is a very difficult language to translate into any European language, particularly English. All the means of expression—diction, sound and rhythm – are different. Only finding authentic English equivalents for words, sounds, and rhythms in Bengali and, above all, the emotional values could render him successfull.

While doing the translations I was conscious of the rhyming scheme, diction, sound and rhythm of original Bengali poems. I knew it would be impossible to maintain them all and I must choose. I have maintained the end rhymes of all the poems same as those used by Rabindranath. Also my emphasis has been finding authentic English equivalents of words and phrases. In selecting poems I came across many words for which there seemed no English equivalents with even approximate emotional values. I avoided translating them. In a way I did not choose the poems in this collection. The poems chose me. I found that maintaining the sounds were most difficult. Sound in Rabindranath's poems means music. His poems are lyrical and they sing. Songs are specific to a culture and to its people. Songs can not be translated into *songs* in another language. I tried to write them as English verse with consistent rhythm within the poems.

There are many Bengali words, particularly names, in the translations. I have written them in Roman script following the "unofficial standard" ways Bengalis write them. English meaning of these words are in the glossary of words. But in the transliteration of the Bengali poems I have used the international convention for Sanskrit transliteration.

The poem, Awakening of the Waterfall (*Nirjharer Svapnabhanga*), was taken from the popular anthology of Rabindranath in Bengali, *Sanchaita*. All other poems in this collection are from *Rabindra Racanabali, Vols. I, II and III,* Centenary Edition published by the Government of West Bengal, 1961.

I have no illusions that I have all the necessary qualifications as a translator. I did not seek the unattainable goal of achieving perfection. Instead, I sought to keep loss of quality of the originals to a minimum. My work may not meet the rigorous expectations of scholars and critics but they may satisfy the appetite of poetry lovers a little. To the scholars I want to say that Rabindranath in his translation from Sanskrit to Bengali in *Rupantar* or in his translations of his own works in English he has favoured 'transcreation' rather than translation (for example, *Gitanjali* and Red Oleanders).

I hope that others will take up the task of translation of Rabindranath's works, including the ones presented here. The reading public should have many options and choose the one they like best.

Jadu Saha
Ottawa, Canada

Śandhyāsaṃgit, 1882

Śiśir

Śiśir kāṁdiā śudhu bale,
"Kena mor hena kṣudra prāṇ–
Śiśuṭir kalpanār mato
Janami amani abasān?
Ghum–bhañga uṣā–meyeṭir
Ekṭi sukher aśru hāy,
Hāsi tār phurāte phurāte
E aśruti śukāiyā jāy.
Ṭukṭuke mukhkhani niye
Golāp hāsiche muchkiye,
Bakul prāṇer sudhā diye,
Bayure mātāl kari tule–
Prajāpaṭi bhābiya nā pāy
Kāhāre tāhār parān cāy,
Tuliyā alas pākhā duṭi
Bhramiteche phul hate phule–
Sei hāsi rāśir mājhāre
Āmi kena thākite nā pāi.
Jemani nayan meli hāy,
Sukher nimeṣṭir prāy,
Atripta hāsiṭi mukhe laye
Amani kemane go mare jāi."
Śuye śuye aśok–pātāy
Mumurṣu śiśir bale "Hāy,
Kono sukh phurāy ni jār
Tār keno jiban phurāy?"

Evening Songs, 1882

The Dew-drop

Weeping, wails the dew-drop,
"Why is my life so short
Like a child's fancy, as
It's born it comes to naught?
A contented tear-drop
Of awakened Dawn,
Alas! it always dries before
All her smile is gone.
With her glorious red lips
The rose smiles happily;
Giving her life's nectar
Bakul fuddles the world madly;
'The butterfly does not know
For whom its heart hungers,
Sailing on its lazy wings
From flower to flower it flutters.
Why is it that I cannot live
For ever, in the midst of this
Mirth! As I open my eyes,
Like a wink of sublime bliss,
With the unspent smile on my lips
Why do I fall into death's grip?"
Lying on the fresh green leaf
The dying dewdrop wails,

"Alas, when my bliss isn't over

"Ami bali kena haini śiśir?"
Kahe kabi niśvās pheliyā.
"Prabhātei jetām śukāye
Prabhātei nayan meliyā.
Hey bidhātā, śiśirer mato
Garecha āmār ei prāṇ,
Śiśirer maranṭi kena
Āmāre karoni tabe dān?"

❄ ❄ ❄ ❄ ❄

Why does my life fail?"
"Why was I not a dewdrop?'
The poet says with a sigh;
"In the morning I would have
Opened my eyes, then die.
O God, like a dewdrop
You made this life of mine
Why did you not keep my
Death also in its confine?"

❄❄❄❄❄

Prabhātsaṃgit, 1883

Nirjharer svapnabhanga

Āji e prabhāte rabir kar
Kemane paśila prāner par,
Kemane paśila guhār āṁdhāre prabhātpākhir gān
Na jāni kena re eta din pare jāgiyā uṭhila prān.
Jāgiyā uṭhiche prān,
Ore uthali uṭheche bari,
Ore prāner bāsanā prāner ābeg rudhiyā rākhite nāri.
Thar thar kari kāṁpiche bhudhar,
Śilā rāśi rāśi paḍiche khase,
Phuliyā phuliyā phenila salil
Garaji uṭhiche dāruṇ roṣe.
Hethāy hothāy pāgaler prāy
Ghuriyā ghuriyā mātiyā beḍāy–
Bāhirite cāy dekhite nā pāy kothāy kārār dvār.
Kena re bidhātā pāṣān hena,
Cāri dike tār bāṁdhan kena
Bhāng re hṛday bhāng re bāṁdhan,
Sādh re ājike prāṇer sādhaṇ
Laharir pare lahari tuliyā
Āghāter par āghāt kar.
Mātiyā jakhan uṭhiche parān
Kiser āṁdhār kiser pāṣān
Uthali jakhan uṭhiche bāsanā
Jagate takhan kiser ḍar.

Āmi dhāliba karunādhārā
Āmi bhāngiba paṣān kārā,
Āmi jagat plābiyā beḍāba gāhiyā
Ākul pāgal pārā.
Keś elāiyā, phul kuḍāiyā,
Ramdhanu–āṁkā pākhā uḍāiyā,

Morning Songs, 1883

Awakening of the Waterfall

The sunbeams in this morning
How on my heart they're shining?
In the dark cave how entered the morning birds' song?
I don't know why my heart awakens after so long
And awakens life along.
O gushes out water
O my heart's desire, zest for life holds no bar.
The mountain is trembling,
Fallen rocks are piling,
Swollen water is foaming,
In fierce rage they're roaring.
Like mad it wanders here,
Meanders over there
Wants to get out but finds not the prison-door.
Why is god like the stone?
Why are there chains alone?
Break the bond, break the heart,
In quest for life I must start:
Wave after wave raising
Again and again striking.
Flying is now life's spark
Fear not rocks, fear not dark.
When will is surging here
In this world there is no fear.

A stream of kindness I'll pour
I'll break the prison's stone-door.
Flooding the earth I will sing
And roam like a mad being.
Spreading my tresses, gathering flowers,
Flying on my wings of rainbow-colours,

Rabir kiraṇe hāsi chaḍāiyā diba re parān dhāli.
Śikhar haiyete śikhare chuṭiba,
Bhūdhar haiyete bhūdhare luṭiba,
Hese khalkhal geye kalkal tāle tāle diba tāli.
Eta kathā āche eta gān āche, eta prān āche mor,
Eta sukh āche, eta sādh āche – prān haye āche bhor.
Ki jāni ki hala āji, jagiyā uṭhila prāṇ–
Dur hate śuni jena mahāsāgarer gān.
Ore, cāri dike mor
E ki kārāgār ghor–
Bhāng bhāng bhāng kārā, āghāte āghāt kar.
Ore, āj ki gān geyeche pākhi,
Eseche rabir kar.

❄❄❄❄❄

Scattering my smile in the sunbeam
My heart will be pouring in the stream.
    From peak to peak I'll run
    From mount to mount I'll turn
    Roaring with laughter, babbling songs,
    I'll clap with its rhythm life long.
So much to say, so much to sing, so much life is within!
So much joy, so much desire – my heart is full to the brim!
I don't know why my heart awakens after so long!
From very far away as I hear the ocean's song.
    O why the dungeon besiege me
    And darkness around it shall be?
With blow after blow, blow after blow
Break and open this prison's woe.
O what songs do the birds sing today
    And comes now the sun's ray.

❄ ❄ ❄ ❄ ❄

Chabi O Gān, 1883

Ekākini

Ekṭi meye ekelā,
Sāṁjher belā,
Māṭh diye caleche.
Cāri dike sonār dhān phaleche.
Or mukhete paḍeche sāṁjher ābhā,
Culete kariche jhikimiki.
Ke jāne ki bhābe mane mane
Anmane cale dhikidhiki.
Paścime sonāy sonāmay,
Eta sonā ke kothā dekheche.
Tāri mājhe malin meyeṭi
Ke jena re eṁke rekheche.
Mukhkhāni kena go aman dhārā,
Konkhāne hayeche pathahārā
Kāre jena ki kathā sudhābe,
Sudhāite bhaye hay sārā.
Caran calite bādhe bādhe,
Sudhāle kathāṭi nahi kay.
Baḍo baḍo ākul nayane
Śudhu mukhapāne ceye ray.
Nayan kariche chalchal,
Ekhani paḍibe jena jal.
Sāṁjhete nirālā sab ṭhāi,
Māṭhe kothao janaprāṇi nāi–
Dūre ati dūre dekhā jāy,
Malin se sāṁjher ālote
Chāyā chāyā gāchpālāguli
Meśe meśe megher kolete.

Picture and Song, 1883

Alone

One girl alone, in the evening,
Through the meadow she's passing.
All around is ready
The golden paddy.
On her face is the sunset's glow.
What's on her mind, I don't know.
On her tresses the glow is shining.
So absently, slowly she is walking.
In the west is gold upon gold,
Too much golden beauty to behold!
Amidst that someone has drawn
The girl so wan.
Why is her face like so today,
Where did she lose her way?
She wants to ask something
But enough courage she can't bring.
With hesitant steps is her movement.
When asked something she remains silent.
With big eyes imploring and needy
She only keeps looking at me.
Her moist eyes are now shimmering
As if tears will now begin flowing.
All are desolate at this twilight
Even a single soul is not in sight.
Far, so distant, I can see
Shadowy lines of forest trees
Being kissed by clouds so light
As the evening turns to night.

Baḍo tor bājiteche pāy,
Āye re āmār kole āye.
Ā mari jananī tor ke,
    Bal re kothāy tor ghar.
Tarāse cāhis kena re,
    Āmāre bāsis kena par.

❄ ❄ ❄ ❄ ❄

Your feet must be hurting.
Come to my lap for resting.
Oh, where's the one that gave you birth
  And where's your home upon this earth?
Why is this look of wonder?
  Why take me as a stranger?

❄ ❄ ❄ ❄ ❄

Kaḍi O Komal, 1886

Prāṇ

Marite cāhi nā āmi sundar bhubane,
Mānaber mājhe āmi bāṁcibāre cāi.
Ei sūryakare ei puspita kānane
Jibanta hṛday mājhe yadi sthān pāi.
Dharāy prāner khelā cira tarangita,
Biraha milan kata hāsi aśrumay,
Mānaber sukhe duḥkhe gāṁthiā sangīt
Yadi go rachite pāri amar ālay.
Tā yadi nā pāri tabe bāṁci yata kāl
Tomāderi mājhkhāne labhi yena ṭhāi,
Tomrā tulibe bale sakāl bikāl
Naba naba sangīter kusum phuṭāi.
Hāsimukhe nio phul, tār pare hāy
Phele dio phul, yadi se phul śukāy.

❄ ❄ ❄

Ākāṅkṣā

Āji śarat–tapane prabhat–svapane
Ki jāni parān ki ye cāy.
Oi śephalir śākhe ki baliā dāke
Bihaga–bihagī ki ye gāy.
Āji madhur bātaṣe hṛday udāse
Rahe nā ābāse mana hāy.
Kon kusumer āśe, kon phulabāse
Sunil ākāṣe man dhāy.
Āji ke yena go nāi e prabhāte tāi
Jīban biphal hay go.

Sharps and Flats, 1886

Life

From this lovely world I don't want to part
Among humanity I want to be living
I yearn to abide in living hearts
Amidst sunshine and flowering gardens thriving.
In this world life's play is ever surging:
Amidst parting, meeting, tears and laughter
I can weave songs with man's joy and grieving
And can make a place for here and after.
If that can't be then as long as I'm here
Among you may I have a place for living.
I'll make a flower of song for your cheer
Bloom in every morning and in evening.
With a smile, my flowers, you may gather
And throw them out, alas, if they wither.

❄ ❄ ❄

Longing

In this sunny, dreamy autumn morning
    Don't know what my mind is seeking
And on that *shephali* bough I don't know any how
    What the bird-pair is singing.
Listless is my heart in sweetness the breeze impart
    And my mind is restless,
Hoping for which flower, in which bower
    My mind flies to the sky's blueness?

Tāi cāridike cāy man keṁde gāy
"E nahe, e nahe, nay go."
Kon svapaner deśe āche elokeśe,
Kon chāyāmayi amarāy.
Āji kon upabane biraha bedane
Āmāri kārane kāṁde hāy.
Āmi yadi gāṁthi gān athir parāṇ
Se gān śunāba kāre ār.
Āmi yadi gāṁthi mālā laye phuladāla
Kahāre parāba phulahār.
Āmi āmār e prān yadi kari dān
Diba prāṇ tabe kār pāy.
Sada bhay hay mane pāche ajatane
Mane mane keha bythā pāy.

❄ ❄ ❄ ❄ ❄

Vain is my living in this morning
Because someone I miss
So I search about and my heart cries out
"Not this, not this, O not this!"
With her unbound tresses, in which dreamland's recesses
Or shadowy heaven is she abiding,
And for the agony of parting from me
In which forest is she weeping?
If a song I string with my yearning
Shall I sing it for whom?
To whom shall I give if a garland I weave
From a basket of bloom
If I want to tender my heart as an offer
At whose feet I'll be doing?
Always I'm frightened lest being negligent
I hurt someone's feeling.

❄ ❄ ❄ ❄ ❄

Mānasi, 1890

Śrānti

Kata bār mane kari pūrṇimāniśīthe
Snigdha samiran,
Nidralas āṁkhi–sama dhīre yadi mude āse
E śrānta jiban.
Gaganer animeṣ jagrata cāṁder pāne
Mukta duṭi bātāyandvār—
Sudūre prahar bāje, gangā kothā bahe cale
Nidrāy suṣupta dui pār.
Mājhi gān geye yāy brindābangāthā
Āpanār mane,
Cirajibaner smṛti aśru haye gale āse
Nayaner kone.
Svapner sudhīr srote dūre bhese yāy prān
Svapna hate niḥsvapna atale,
Bhāsān pradīp yathā nibe giye sandhyābāye
Ḍube yāy janhabīr jale.

❄❄❄❄❄

She Who is in the Mind, 1890

Weariness

In the soft breeze and full moon night
  The thought oft comes to me —-
As droops the eyelids in slumber
    Should this drained life's end be.
The two doors of the window are opened
    To the unblinking moon in the sky,
Far away the clock strikes, with banks deep asleep
    The Ganges is flowing by.
The boatman goes singing to himself
    Old minstrel song,
Melts into tears in the eyes
    The memories lifelong.
Floats life in the stream of dream
    To the dreamless deep
As sinks the floating lamp in river
    Snuffed out by the wind's whip.

❄❄❄❄❄

Sonār tari, 1894

Sonār tari

Gagane garaje megh ghana baraṣā.
Kule ekā base āchi nāhi bharasā.
  Rāśi Rāśi bhārā bhārā
  Dhān kātā hala sārā,
  Bharānadi kṣuradhārā
    Kharaparaśā.
Kāṭite kaṭite dhān ela baraṣā.

Ekkhāni choto khet, āmi ekelā,
Cāri dike bāṁkā jal kariche khelā.
  Parapāre dekhi āṁkā
  Taruchāyāmasimākhā
  Grāmkhāni meghe ḍhākā
    Prabhātbela—
E pārete choṭo khet āmi ekelā.

Gān geye tari beye ke āse pāre,
Dekhe yena mane hay cini uhāre.
  Bharā pāle cale yāy,
  Kono dike nāhi cāy,
  Dheuguli nirupāy
    Bhānge du dhāre—
Dekhe yena mane hay cini uhāre.

Ogo, tumi kothā yāo kon bidesé,
Bārek bhiḍāo tari kulete ese
  Yeo yethā yete cāo,
  Yāre khuśi tāre dāo,
  Śudhu tumi niye yāo
    Kṣaṇik hese
Āmār sonār dhān kulete ese.

The Golden Boat, 1894

Golden Boat

In the heavens, clouds rumble; rain is endless.
On the bank I sit, all alone and hopeless.
    Harvest has ended — sheaves are piled high.
    Now the swollen river flows fiercely by.
While cutting the paddy, the rain was ceaseless.

One small paddy field — no one but me.
Swirling tide is all that I see.
    Trees like ink-smears on the bank far away.
    Village, overcast in the morn, seems painted gray.
On this bank, one small field and no one but me.

Who is this, singing and steering to shore?
I think it's someone from days of yore.
    In full-sail, eyes fixed ahead, he's moving.
    On both sides, relentless waves breaking.
Watching I feel I've seen him before.

Oh to what foreign land are you heading?
Moor your boat for a while before going.
    Go where you want to, give who you please,
    But come to this bank, come smile, be at ease
And take my golden sheaves before leaving.

Yata cāo tata lao taranī–pare.
Ār āche? –ār nāi, diyechi bhare.
    Etakāl nadikule
    Yāhā laye chinu bhule
    Sakali dilām tule
        Thare bithare—
Ekhan āmāre laha karunā kare.

Ṭhai nāi, thāi nāi — choṭo se tarī
Āmāri sonār dhāne giyeche bhari.
    Śrabangagan ghire
    Ghana megh ghure phire
    Śunya nadīr tīre
        Rahinu paḍi—
Yāhā chila niye gela sonār tarī.

❄❄❄

Māyābād

Hā re nirānanda deś, pari jirna jarā,
Bahi bigñatār bojhā, bhābitecha mane—
Iśvarer prabañcanā pariyāche dharā
Sucatur sukṣadṛṣṭi tomār nayane
Laye kushānkur buddhi śāṇita prakharā
Karmahin ratridin basi grihakone
Mithyā bale janiācha biśvabasundharā
Grahatāramay sṛṣṭi ananta gagane.
Yugyugāntar dhare paśu pakṣi prāṇī
Acal nirbhaye hethā niteche niśvās
Bidhātār jagatere matṛkroḍ māni;
Tumi bṛdha kichurei kara nā biśvās
Lakṣa koṭi jiba laye e biśver melā;
Tumi jānitecha mane, sab chelekhelā.

❄❄❄

Take them all, take as much as you can load.
Are there more? No, none, I placed all aboard.
    What bewitched me, here by the river —-
    I've loaded all, layer by layer.
Now take me too, be kind, take me aboard.

No room, no room any more, the boat is too small.
The sheaves of my golden paddy have filled it all.
    Across the *Sraban* sky heavy clouds ply,
    On the empty bank alone I stand by –
What I had is gone: the golden boat took it all.

❄ ❄ ❄

On the Doctrine Maya

Ah my joyless country, in tattered decrepit dress,
Loaded with your own sagacity, you're thinking
That you have uncovered God's deception process
By your all too-clever gaze discriminating.
With your wit as sharp as a needle of the *kush*-grass,
Unemployed, in your home you sit in confusion
Convinced you are that this world, this vast universe,
Planets and stars in the endless sky are but illusion.
For aeons, birds and beasts and other living things
Bereft of unshakeable fear, all are breathing here.
God's world is mother's lap to all other beings,
But you, old dotard, believe in nothing that's near.
And this cosmic playground of billions of living
Beings is to you only child's play, meaning nothing.

❄ ❄ ❄

Nadipathe

Gagan ḍhākā ghana meghe.
Paban bahe khara bege.
  Aśani jhanajhana
  Dhvaniche ghana ghana
Nadīte ḍheu uṭhe jege.
Paban bahe khara bege.

Tīrete taruraji dole
Ākul marmara–role.
  Cikura cikimike
  Cakiyā dike dike
Timira ciri yāy cale.
Tirete taruraji dole.

Jhariche bādaler dhārā
Birām biśrām hārā.
  Bārek theme āse,
  Dviguṇ ucchāse
Ābār pāgaler pārā
Jhariche bādaler dhārā.

Meghete patharekhā līn,
Prahar tāi gatihīn.
  Gaganpāne cāi
  Jānite nahi pāi
Geche ki nāhi geche din.
Prahar tāi gatihīn.

Tīrete bāṁdhiāchi tarī,
Rayechi sārādin dhari.
  Ekhano path nāki
  Anek āche bāki,
Āsiche ghor bibhābarī.
Tīrete bāṁdhiāchi tarī.

On the River

Overcast is the sky,
The wind is blowing high,
    Rolls the thunder,
    Over and over,
Waves swell in the river nigh,
The wind is blowing high.

On the banks trees sway listless.
With murmuring so endless,
    And flashes lightning,
    All around startling,
Blazing and piercing darkness.
On the banks trees sway listless.

Torrents of rain are pouring,
Without abating or ceasing;
    If ever shows weakening,
    Start again with force doubling.
Like mad again it's coming,
Torrents of rain are pouring.

In darkness the road is fading.
That's why the time seems unmoving.
    Looking at the sky
    I can't verify
If at last the day is ending.
That's why the time seems unmoving.

To the shore the boat is tied,
All day long here I abide,
    A long way for travelling
    It seems is still remaining,
Comes the deep dark night,
To the shore the boat is tied.

Basiā taraṇ̄ir kone
Ekelā bhābi mane mane—
    Mejhete sej pāti
    Se āji jāge rāti,
Nidrā nāhi dunayane.
Basiyā bhābi mane mane.

Megher dāk śune kāṁpe,
Hṛday dui hāte cāṁpe.
    Ākāś pāne cāy,
    Bharasā nāhi pāy,
Tarāse sārā niśi yāpe,
Megher ḍāk śune kāṁpe.

Kabhu bā bāyubegabhare
Duār jhanajhani paḍe.
    Pradip nibe āse
    Chāyati kāṁpe trāse,
Nayane āṁkhijal jhare
Bakṣa kāṁpe tharathare.

Cakita āṁkhi duṭi tār
Mane āsiche bār bār.
    Bahire mahā jhaḍ
    Bajra kaḍamaḍ,
Ākāś kare hāhākār.
Mane paḍiche āṁkhi tār.

Gagan ḍhākā ghana meghe,
Paban bahe khara bege.
    Aśani jhanajhana
    Dhvaniche ghana ghana,
Nad̄ite dheu uṭhe jege.
Pabana bahe āji bege.

*****

Sitting in the boat's corner
All alone I do ponder
  With a lantern's light
  She is awake through the night
With sleepless eyes here
I sit and ponder.

Trembling at thunder's rumbling,
With hands her heart she's clasping,
  The sky at a distance,
  Offers no assurance,
In fear the night she is spending
And trembling at thunder rumbling.

At times the wind is raging.
Making the door teetering,
  The lantern flickers,
  The shadow shivers,
Her eyes rain tears,
And her heart shivers.

Her two eyes frightened
Come to mind often.
  Outside the storm is raging,
  The thunderclaps are roaring,
The sky is in despair,
Her eyes I remember.

Overcast is the sky,
The wind blows high,
  Rolls the thunder,
  Over and over,
Waves swell in the river nigh,
The wind is blowing high.

❄ ❄ ❄ ❄ ❄

Citrā, 1896

Svarga haite bidāy

Mlān haye ela kaṇṭhe mandārmālikā,
Hey mahendra, nirbāpita jyotirmay tikā
Malin lalāte. Punyabal hala kṣin,
Āji mor svarga hate bidāyer din
Hey deb, hey debigan. Barṣa lakṣasato
Yāpan karechi harṣe debatār mato
Debaloke. Āji seṣ biccheder kṣaṇe
Leṣ mātra aśrurekha svarger nayane
Dekhe yāba ei āśā chila. Śokhīn
Hṛdihīn sukhasvargabhumi, udāsīn
Ceye āche. Lakṣa lakṣa barṣa tār
Cakṣer palak nahe; Aśvatha śākhār
Prānta hate khasi gele jirṇatama pātā
Yataṭuku bāje tār, tataṭuku byāthā
Svarge nāhi lāge, yabe morā śato śato
Grihacyuta hatajyoti nakṣtrer mato
Muhurte khasiā paḍi debalok hate
Dharitrīr antahīn janmamṛtyu srote.
Se bedanā bajita yadyapi, biraher
Chāyārekhā dita dekhā, tabe svarger
Cirajyoti mlān hata martyer matan
Komal śiśirbāṣpe — nandankānan

Marmariā uthita niśvasi, mandakinī
Kule kule geye yeta karun kāhinī
Kalakaṇṭhe, sandhyā āsi dibā abasāne
Nirjan prantar–pare diganter pāne
Cale yeta udāsinī, nistabdha niśīth
Jhillimantre śunāita bairāgyasangit
Nakṣatra sabhāy. Mājhe mājhe surapure

The Multi-coloured, 1896

Farewell To Heaven

Now withers the garland of *mandar* flowers around my neck.
O great *Indra,* the radiance of the mark that did bedeck
Is gone from my sullied forehead. The strength of my piety
Wanes. O gods, goddesses, today I must bid to your society
My farewell. Many millennia gladly did I stay
Like a god in the kingdom of gods and on this day
Of parting a trace of tears in heaven's eye I hoped to see,
But in this griefless, heartless, detached, happy land that's not to be.
It just looks on. To its eye millennia's passing
Is not a blink; for heaven doesn't have as much hurt feeling
As the branch of a *peepul*-tree does at the falling
Of the driest leaf when hundreds of us human beings
Like burnt out homeless stars are lost from gods' sanctum
To the earth's endless stream of births and deaths' realm.
And should such hurt have been felt, separation's shadow
Would have fallen across heaven, its eternal glow
Would have been dimmed with soft dewy vapour as on earth.
Nandan-garden would have whispered sighs and not mirth.

Flowing *Mandakini* would sing sad tales.
At the day's end, evening would come and veil
Slowly over the far end of the lonely field to the horizon.
In still night the crickets' stoical chanting would have risen
Under the assembled stars. Dancing *Menaka*'s golden anklets,

Nṛtyaparā menakār kanaknupure
Tāl bhanga hata. Heli urbasīr stane
Svarṇabinā theke theke yena anyamane
Akasmāt jhaṁkārita kaṭhin pīḍane
Nidārun karuṇ murchanā. Dita dekhā
Debatār aśruhīn cokhe jalarekhā
Niṣkāraṇe. Patipāśe basi ekāsane
Sahasā cāhita śacī indrer nayane
Yena khuṁji pipāsār bāri. Dharā hate
Mājhe mājhe ucchasi āsita bāyusrote
Dharanir sudirgha niśvās —khasi jhari
Paḍita nandan bane kusumamanjarī.

Thāko svarga hāsyamukhe, karo sudhāpān
Debagan. Svarga tomāderi sukhasthān—
Morā parabasi. Martyabhumi svarga nahe,
Se ye mātribhumi— tāi tār cakṣe bahe
Aśrujaladhārā, yadi du diner pare
Keha tāre ceḍe yāy du dander tare.
Yata kṣudra, yata kṣin, yata abhājan,
Yata pāpītāpī, meli bygra alingan
Sabāre komal bakṣe bāṁdhibāre cāy—
Dhūlimākhā tanusparśe hṛday juḍāy
Jananīr. Svarge taba bahuk amṛta,
Martye thāk sukhe duḥkhe anantamiśrita
Premadhārā— aśrujale ciraśyama kari
Bhūtaler svargakhaṇḍaguli.
Hey apsarī,
Tomār nayanjyoti premabedanāy
Kabhu nā hauk mlān— lainu bidāy.
Tumi kāre karo nā prārthanā, kāro tare
Nāhi śok. Dharātale dīnatama ghare
Yadi janme preyesī āmār, nadītīre
Kono–ek gramaprānte pracchanna kutire

At times would have missed a beat; leaning on *Urvashi's* breast,
At times, her golden harp-strings carelessly roughly pressed
Suddenly would have burst into doleful music digressed.
Shimmer of tears might have appeared then
On the dry eyes of the gods. Suddenly when
Seated on the same seat by her husband's side,
As if seeking water for her thirst, *Shachi* might
Look at *Indra's* eyes. The wind might have wafted high
Towards heaven gusts of the earth's long-drawn sigh
Shaking flowers off the *Nandan* branches nigh.
Stay in mirth, Heaven. Gods, drink your nectar.
Heaven is indeed your place of bliss hereafter
Where we are aliens. Earth – she is no heaven,
But she is a motherland; so her eyes are laden
With raining tears, if after a few days anyone
Leaves her even for a few hours. The trifling one,
The meek, the forlorn, the sick and the suffering —
All she holds tight to her breast in embrace of yearning.
Mother is content with her sullied children's touch
So let nectar flow in heaven, and love as such,
Streaming on earth mixed with pain and pleasure, tears
Keep the earth's heaven-spots tender and green forever.

O nymph, may the sparkle of your ever bright eye
Never subside. It is time to bid you goodbye.
You desire none, nor grieve for any. Should my lover
Be born in the humblest home on earth, by the river,

Aśvatthachayāy, se bālikā bakṣe tār
Rakhibe sancay kari sudhār bhāṇḍar
Āmāri lāgiya sayatane. Śiśukāle
Nadīkule śibamūrti gaḍiā sakāle
Āmāre māgiā labe bar. Sandhyā hale
Jvalanta pradipkhāni bhāsāiā jale
Śankita kampita bakṣe cāhi ekmanā
Karibe se āpnār saubhāgya gananā
Ekākī dāṁḍāe ghāte. Ekadā sukṣane
Āsibe āmār ghare sannata nayane
Candancarcita bhāle raktapaṭṭāmbare,
Utsaber bāṁśari sangīte. Tār pare
Sudine durdine, kalyānkankaṇ kare,
Sīmantasīmāy mangalsindurbindu,
Gṛha lakṣmi duḥkhe sukhepūrnimār indu
Saṃsārer samudraśiare. Debgan,
Mājhe mājhe ei svarga haibe smaran
Dūr svapnasama, yabe kono ardharāte
Sahasā heriba jāgi nirmal sajyāte
Paḍeche candrer ālo, nidritā preyasi,
Lunthita śithil bāhu, paḍiāche khasi
Granthi saramer— mṛdu sohāgcumbane
Sacakite jagi uṭhi gāḍha ālingane
Latāibe bakṣe mor— dakṣina anil
Ānibe phuler gandha, jagrata kokil
Gahibe sudur śākhe.
Ai Dīnahīnā,
Aśru–āṁkhi duḥkhaturā jananī malinā
Ai mātṛbhumi. Āji bahudin pare
Kāndiā uṭheche citta tor tare.
Yemani bidāyduḥkhe śuṣka dui cokh
Aśrute purila, amni e svargalok
Alas kalpanāprāy kothāy milālo
Chāyāchchabi. Taba nilākās, taba ālo
Taba janapurna lokālay, sindhutīre

In a hut half-hidden in the shade of a *peepul*-tree,
With care she would gather in her breast love's nectar for me.
As a child, sitting on the river-bank in the morning
She will fashion Shiva's image with clay and be praying
To have me as her bridegroom. When evening draws near,

All alone on the *ghat,* her heart quivering with fear
She'll light a lamp and let it float on the river
And with total concentration she will ponder
Her fortunes. Then one day at an hour opportune,
She will come with the playing of flute's festive tune
Into my home; draped in red silk, her eyes lowered
And sandal-paste tracery on her forehead bared.

In days of joy and sorrow with her bangles auspicious,
Below her parted hair the vermilion dot propitious,
She will be the living goddess of my home, refulgent,
Calm like the full moon over the world-ocean in torment.
Sometimes, gods, I'll recall this heaven like a far-off dream
When halfway through the night, waking up I'll see the moonbeam
Flooding the white bed where my beloved is sleeping,
Limp arms lying loosely, sari unkempt, having
Forgotten shyness. Suddenly roused by my kisses tender,
She will hold me in firm embrace and twine like a creeper
Around my chest, as the south wind wafts flower fragrance
And a *koel*, wide-awake, sings from a distant branch.

Ah, indigent, afflicted, tearful, sullied mother,
After so many ages today my heart does quiver
With cries for you. As soon as the sadness of parting
Filled these dry eyes with tears this heaven was vanishing
Like an idle-dream or a shadow play. Your blue sky, your light,

Sudīrgha balukātaṭ, nil giriśire
Śubhra himarekhā, taruśreṇīr mājhāre
Niḥśabda aruṇoday, sunya nadīpāre
Abanatamukhī sandhyā— bindūaśrujale
Yata pratibimba yena darpaner tale
Paḍeche khasiā.
Hey jananī putrahārā,
Śeṣ biccheder dine ye śokāśrudhārā
Cakṣu hate jhare paḍi taba mātṛstan
Karechila abhisikta, āji etakṣan
Se aśru śukāye geche. Tabu jānī mane
Yakhani phiriba puna taba niketane
Takhani dukhāni bāhu dharibe āmāy,
Bajibe maṅgalśankha, sneher chāyāy
Duḥkhe sukhe bhaye bharā premer saṁsāre
Taba gehe, taba putrakanyār mājhāre,
Āmāre laibe ciraparicitasama—
Tār pardin hate śiyarete mama
Sārākṣan jāgi rabe kampamān prāṇe,
Śankita antare, ūrdhe debatār pāne
Meliā karuṇ dṛṣṭi, cintita sadāi
Yāhāre peyechi tāre kakhan hārāi.

❄ ❄ ❄

Urbaśī

Naha mātā, naha kanyā naha badhū sundari rupaśī,
Hey nandanabāsinī urbaśī.
Gosṭhe yabe sandhyā nāme śrānta dehe svārnāncala ṭāni
Tumi kona gṛha prānte nāhi jvālo sandhyādīpakhāni,
Dvidhāy jaḍita pade kamprabakṣe namranetrapāte
Smitahāsye nāhi cala salajjita bāsarśajyāte
Stabhda ardharāte.
Uṣār uday sama anabagunthitā

Your teeming habitations, long sandy beaches bright
By the sea, on the heads of blue mountains white snow's linings,
Silent sunrise between rows of trees, face-lowered evenings
On deserted river-banks – all were in a drop of tear —
Reflections within a mirror.

Ah, sonless mother,
The rain of tears you shed at our last parting,
Which, welling from your two eyes overflowing Anointed your
maternal breasts, has now dried up. Even so,
In my mind I do know when to your abode I shall go.
Once more, instantly you'll hold me in embrace sweet.
The good-omen conch-shells will sound and you will greet
Me as one long known to you. I'll be in love's nest.
Your home, with pain, pleasure, fear, children and love blessed
From the next day I know you'll be at my bedside, eyes alert,
And with an apprehensive and fluttering heart,
Sad gaze upturned to the gods above, and wondering
That the one you have gained when you might be losing.

❄ ❄ ❄

Urvashi

Not mother, nor daughter, nor a wife you are to be,
O paradise dweller, ravishing Urvashi.
When on the meadow does the evening descend
Draping round your tired shape with garment's golden end
In any home the evening lamp you do not light;
With faltering steps, trembling heart and downcast sight,
Smiling and blushing to the bridal bed you do not pass
In midnight's hush.
Unveiled as the rise of dawn
Unashamedly you adorn.

Tumi akuṇṭhitā.
Bṛntahīn puspasama apanate āpani bikaśi
Kabe tumi phuṭile urbaśī.
Ādim basantaprāte uṭhechile manthita sāgare
Dān hāte sudhāpātra biṣabhāṇḍa laye bāmkare,
Tarangita mahāsindhu mantraśānta bhujaṅger mato
Paḍechila padaprānte ucchvasita phaṇā lakṣa śata
Kari abanata.
Kundaśubhra nagnakanti surendrabanditā
Tumi aninditā.

Konokāle chile nā ki mukulikā balikā bayasī
Hey anantayoubanā urbaśi.
Āṁdhār pāthārtale kār ghare basiā ekelā
Mānik mukutā laye karechile śaiśaber khelā,
Maṇidīpadīpta kakṣesamudrer kallolsaṁgīte
Akalanka hāsya mukhe prabāl pālaṅke ghumāite
Kār aṅkaṭite.
Yakhani jāgile biśve, youbangaṭhitā
Purṇaprasphuṭitā.

Yugyugāntar hate tumi śudhu bisver preyasī
Hey apūrba śobhanā urbaśī.
Munigaṇ dhyān bhāṅgi dey pade tapasyār phal,
Tomāri kaṭākṣaghāte tribhuban youbancancal,
Tomār madir gandha andhabayu bahe cāribhite,
Madhumatta bhṛngasama mugdha kabi phire lubdha cite
Uddām sangīte.
Nupur gunjari yāo ākul–añcalā
Bidyutcañcalā.

Surasabhātale yabe nṛtya kara pulake ullasi
Hey bilolhillol urbaśī,
Chande chande nāci uṭhe sindhumājhe taranger dal,
Śasyaśīrṣe śihariā kāṁpi uṭhe dharār añcal,

Blooming like a flower without a stem and free
When did you blossom, Urvashi?
In the primal spring-morn, out of the churned sea you did stand
With the nectar cup in your right, the poison cup in left hand.
The wave-tossed mighty ocean, like a spellbound serpent
With its million heaving hoods bowed at your feet silent.
White as the jasmine undraped resplendence!
The lord of the gods bows in reverence.
O you unblemished radiance!

Were you never tender in age like a maiden budding
O Urvashi, of youth never-ending?
In ocean's dark vault, sitting lone in whose abode
Did you play childhood games with pearls and gems' load?

In a chamber lit by gems' light, to the billowy song of the sea,
With unblemished smiling face, on a coral-cradle, in whose arms it
be That sleepeth thee?
The moment you woke up in this creation
You were in youth's full-bloom fashion.

From aeons past you're the beloved of all on this earth's face
O Urvashi, of incomparable grace.
Saints break their meditation to offer their merit of penance.
Youth stir in the three worlds, struck by the shaft of your glance.
The blind wind blows your intoxicating fragrance all round.
Like a drunken honeybee the poet roams spellbound
With impetuous melody's sound.
Jingling your anklets you go, your garment's end fluttering,
Fast as the lightning.

When you dance in the gods' assembly hall with glee
O swaying, billowing Urvashi!
With that rhythm dances the ocean's surf.
On the heads of crops shivers the earth's scarf.

Taba stanahār hate nabhasthale khasi paḍe tārā—
Akasmāt puruṣer bakṣomājhe citta ātmahārā,
Nāce raktadhārā.
Digante mekhalā taba ṭuṭe acambite
Ayi asambṛte.

Svarger udayācale mūrtimatī tumi hey ūṣasī,
Hey bhubanamohini urbaśī.
Jagater aśrudhāre dhauta taba tanur tanima,
Triloker hṛdirakte āṁkā taba caranaśoṇimā.
Muktabeṇi bibasane, bikaśita biśvabāsanār
Arabinda–mājhkhāne pādapadma rekhecha tomār
Ati laghubhār—
Akhil mānasasvarge anantaranginī,
Hey svapnasanginī.

Oi śuna diśe diśe tomā lāgi kāṁdiche krandasī
Hey nisṭhurā badhirā urbaśī.
Ādiyug purātan e jagate phiribe ki ār,
Atal akūl hate siktakeśe uṭhibe ābār?
Pratham se tanukhāni dekhā dibe pratham prabhāte,
Sarbāṅga kāṁdibe taba nikhiler nayan āghāte
Bāribindupāte—
Akasmat mahambudhi apūrba saṅgite
Rabe taraṅgite.

Phiribe nā, phiribe nā— asta geche se gaurabśaśī,
Astacalabāsinī urbaśī.
Tāi āji dharātale basanter ānanda–ucchvāse
Kār cirabiraher dīrghasvās miśe bahe āse,
Pūrṇimāniśīthe yabe daśa dike paripūrṇa hāsi
Durasmriti kothā hate bājāy byākul karā bāṁśi—
Jhare aśrurāsi.
Tabu āśā jege thāke prāṇer krandane
Ayi abandhane.

* * * * *

The stars fall on sky's floor from the necklace on your breast,
All of a sudden within man's breast his heart knows no rest.
The stream of blood dances in his veins.
Suddenly in the horizon snaps your girdle from its domain,
O you without any restrain.
On heaven's crest of sunrise you're embodied dawn glowing,
O Urvashi, you world-beguiling!

The tears of the world wash your slender form.
Your feet, the glow from creation's heart-blood adorn.
With your tresses unbound, form bare,
On the open lotus of the world's desire
You made the seat for your lotus feet
Ever so light!
In all minds' heaven endless is your delight,
O you mate of the dreams of night!

Hark! Around heaven and earth all are crying for thee,
O cruel, heedless Urvashi!
Will the pristine and ancient age come back to the earth again?
From the boundless deep wet-tressed, will you once more rise
then? Will that form first appear in that first morn?
Hurt by the world's eyes, all your limbs will mourn,
Dripping water from your lovely form.
All of a sudden the great ocean will heave and roar
To a song unsung before.

Never again, never again! That moon of glory has set,
O Urvashi, dwelling in eternal sunset.
On the earth today, the burst of joy of the spring
Is mingled with whose deep sigh of eternal parting!
When laughter is all around in the night of the full moon
From where does the distant memory play its distraught tune?
The tears flow streaming.
Still hope keeps awake in the heart weeping,
O you without bonding!

❄❄❄❄❄

Caitāli, 1898

Debatār bidāy

Debatāmandirmājhe bhakata prabin
Japiteche japamālā basi niśidin.
Henakāle sandhyābelā dhulimākhā dehe
Bastrahīn jirṇadīn paśila se gehe.
Kahila kātarkanṭhe, "gṛha mor nāi,
Ek pāśe dayā kare deho more ṭhāi."
Sasaṃkoce bhaktabar kahilen tāre,
"Āre āre apabitra, dūr haye jā re."
Se kahila, "calilām" — cakṣer nimeṣe
Bhikhāri dharila mūrti debatār beśe.
Bhakta kahe, "prabhu more ki chal chalile."
Debatā kahila, "more dūr kari dile.
Jagate daridrarūpe phiri dayātare,
Gṛhahine gṛha dile āmi thāki ghare."

❄ ❄ ❄

Durlabh janma

Ek din ei dekhā haye yabe śeṣ,
Paḍibe nayanpare antim nimeṣ.
Pardine eimato pohāibe rāt,
Jagrata jagat–pare jāgibe prabhāt.
Kalarabe calibek saṃsārer khelā,
Sukhe duḥkhe ghare ghare bahi yābe belā.
Se kathā smaraṇ kari nikhiler pāne
Āmi āji ceye āchi utsuk nayane.

Chaitra Harvest, 1898

God's Departure

In a temple, day and night an old devotee
While counting beads prayed to his deity.
One such evening a decrepit old man
Covered with dust came for asylum.
In a feeble voice pleaded he, "I have no home,
Please let me stay in a corner of your temple dome."
In biting tone said the great devotee,
"You're unclean, out of this place you must be."
"I'm on my way." So saying, the old beggar,
In a flash, as the deity, did he reappear.
The devotee said, "What a trick you played, my Lord."
The god replied, "Home to me you didn't accord.
Seeking mercy as poor in this world I roam
My home is where the homeless find home."

❄ ❄ ❄

Precious Birth

One day the end will come to my sight.
On my eyes will fall the last light.
Like today, end will come to the next night
With the world waking to a new dawn's light.
The clamour of the world will go on.
In joy and sorrow all will carry on.
Keeping this in mind with eyes keen

Jāhā–kichu heri cokhe kichu tuccha nay,
Sakali durlav bale āji mane hay.
Durlav e dharaṇīr leśatama sthān,
Durlav e jagater byarthatama prān.
Yā pāi ni tāo thāk, yā peyechi tāo,
Tuccha bale yā cāi ni tāi more dāo.

❄❄❄

Pratham cumban

Stabdha hala daśa dik nata kari āṁkhi—
Bandha kari dila gān yata chila pākhi.
Śānta haye gela bāyu, jalakalsvar
Muhurte thamiā gela, baner marmar
Baner marmer mājhe milāila dhīre.
Nistaranga taṭinīr janasúnya tīre
Niḥśabde nāmila āsi sāyāṇnachāyāy
Nistabdha gaganpranta nirbāk dharāy.
Seikṣane bātāyane nīrab nirjan
Āmāder dujaner pratham cumban.
Dik–digantare bāji uṭhila takhani
Debālaye aratir śaṅkha ghaṇṭādvani.
Ananta nakṣtralok uṭhila śihari,
Āmāder cakṣe ela aśrujal bhari.

❄❄❄

Today at the world I'm looking.
Nothing is trivial in what I see.
All is hard to attain, it seems to me.
Precious is a little place on this earth.
Precious is the life that has least worth.
Do not want even what I got or didn't get,
Give me only that, as paltry I didn't covet.

❄ ❄ ❄

The First Kiss

The world became silent with downcast eye—
In a trice stopped the flowing water's lullaby.
Songs of birds stopped; still became the wind's flow.
In the forest's heart died its murmur slow.
On the placid river's desolate shore
In the evening's shadow evermore
Came down the sky's rim soundless
On the earth which was speechless.
Near the window, none around,
We first kissed when it did sound
From far and near conch shell
And peals of temple bells.
Endless stars shivered with thrill
And with tears our eyes did fill.

❄ ❄ ❄

Pallīgrāme

Hethāy tāhāre pāi kāche—
Yata kāche dharātal, yata kāche phulphal—
Yata kāche bāyu jal āche.
Yeman pākhir gān yeman jaler tān
Yemani e prabhater ālo,
Yemani e komalatā, araṇyer śyamalatā,
Temani tāhāre bāsi bhalo.
Yeman sundar sandhyā, yeman rajanīgandhā,
Śuktārā akāśer dhāre,
Yeman se akaluṣā śiśir nirmal uṣā
Temani sundar heri tāre.
Yeman briṣṭir jal yeman akāśtal,
Sukhasupti yeman niśār,
Yeman taṭinīnīr, baṭacchāyā aṭabīr
Temani se mor āpanār.
Yeman nayan bhari aśrujal paḍe jhari
Temani sahaj mor gīti;
Yeman rayeche prāṇ byaptakari marmasthān
Temani rayeche tār prīti.

❄❄❄❄❄

In the Village

Here I feel close to her
The land's closeness, fruits and flowers nearness,
Closeness of air and water.
Like the birds' calling, the river's murmuring,
The gold of the dawn's light,
The softness all around, forest's green unbound,
I love her with the same delight.
As the beautiful evening light, the tuberose perfume at night,
The morning star in the sky,
As unblemished she is as the dew-washed morning is
She is lovely to my eyes.
Like the falling rain, the blue sky's domain,
The deep sleep of the night,
As the river water be, the shade of the *peepul*-tree,
She is my own alright.
As the eye flooding tear comes raining
So come my songs pouring
As there is life in me ever flowing free
Her love for me keeps flowing.

❄❄❄❄❄

Kaṇikā, 1899

Hār–jit

Bhimrule moumāchite hala reṣāreṣi,
Dujanāy mahā tarka kār śakti beśi.
Bhimrul kahe, āche sahasra pramaṇ
Tomār daṃśan nahe āmār samān,
Madhukar niruttar chala chala āṁkhi—
Banadebī kahe tāre kāne kāne dāki,
Kena bāchā nata śir e kathā niścita
Biṣe tumi hār māno, madhute ye jita.

***

Raṣtranīti

Kuḍāl kahila, bhikṣā māgi ogo śāl,
Hātal nāhiko, dāo ekkhāni ḍāl.
Ḍāl niye hātal prastut hala yei,
Tār pare bhikṣuker cāoā cintā nei—
Ekebāre goḍā gheṣe lāgaila kop,
Śāl becārār hala adi anta lop.

*****

Particles, 1899

Defeat and Win

The hornet and the bee were in disagreement.
Who is stronger of the two was the argument.
The hornet said, "Proofs are abounding
You are not my equal in stinging."
The bee remained silent with tear in eye.
The goddess of the forest called him nigh
And whispered, "Why so sad, my sonny?
You lose in venom but surely win in honey."

❄ ❄ ❄

Politics

The axe-blade said, "O tree, I beg thee.
I've no handle. A small branch, please give to me".
As soon as the handle was made from the branch
The beggar forgot his begging at once.
The axe started to strike close to the root
And the poor lost from his head to foot.

❄ ❄ ❄ ❄ ❄

Kṣaṇikā, 1900

Dui tīre

Āmi bhalobāsi āmār
Nadīr bālucar,
Śaratkāle ye nirjane
Cakacakir ghar.

Yethāy phuṭe kāś
Taṭer cāri pāś,
Śīter dine bideśī sab
Hāṁser basabās.

Kacchaperā dhīre
Roudra pohāy tīre,
Du–ekkhāni jeler diṅgi
Sandhyābelāy bhiḍe.

Āmi bhālobāsi āmār
Nadīr bālucar,
Śaratkāle ye nirjane
Cakācakir ghar.

Tumi bhalobāsa tomār
Oi o pārer ban,
Yethāy gāṁthā ghanacchāyā
Pātār ācchādan.

Yethāy bāṁkā gali
Nadīte yāy cali,
Dui dhāre tār beṇubaner
Śākhāy galāgali.

The Flitting One, 1900

Two Shores

To me, the sand beach of
        My river is very dear
Where in the autumn sun
        The curlew birds rear.

Where around the banks
        Catkins grow in number
And in the winter foreign
        Ducks come to slumber.

Slowly the tortoises come
        For basking in the sun
In the dusk a boat or two
        Rests when fishing's done.

To me, the sand beach of
        My river is very dear
Where in the autumn sun
        The curlew birds rear.

You love your wooded forest
        On the other shore
Where dense leaves cast
        Dark shadows on the floor.

Where the meandering lane
        Leads to the river,
And the overhanging reeds
        Clasp each other.

Sakāl sandhyābelā
Ghāṭe badhur melā,
Cheler dale ghaṭer jale
Bhāse bhāsāy bhelā.

Tumi bhalobāsa tomār
Oi o pārer ban,
Yethāy gāṁthā ghanacchāyā
Pātār ācchādan.

Tomār āmār mājhkhānete
Ekti bahe nadī,
Dui taṭere eki gān se
Śonāy nirabadhi.

Āmi śuni śuye,
Bijan bālu–bhuṁeye,
Tumi śono kāṁkher kalas
Ghāṭer pare thuye.

Tumi tāhār gāne
Bojho ekṭā māne,
Āmār kule ār ek artha
Ṭheke āmār kāne.

Tomār āmār mājhkhānete
Ekti bahe nadī,
Dui taṭere ekai gān se
Sonāy nirabadhi.

❄❄❄

In the morn and eve on the quay
Young wives gather.
The boys swim and send their floats
Far down the river.

You love your wooded forest
On the other shore
Where dense leaves cast
Dark shadows on the floor.

Between you and me there is
Only one river,
She sings the same song to
The banks forever.

I listen lying on the
Solitary sand,
You listen setting down the
Pitcher from your hand.

You give one meaning to the
Song of the river
Another meaning comes
To me and strikes my ear.

Between you and me there is
Only one river,
She sings the same song to
The banks forever.

❄❄❄

Śāstra

Pancāśordhve bane yābe
Eman kathā śāstre bale,
Āmrā bali bānaprastha
Youbanetei bhālo cale.
Bane eta bakul phote
Geye mare kokil pākhi,
Latāpātār antarāle
Baḍo saras ḍhākāḍhāki.
Cāṁpār śākhe cāṁder ālo,
Se sṛṣṭi ki kebal miche?
E–sab yārā bojhe tārā
Pancāsater anek nice.
Pancāśordhve bane yābe
Eman kathā śāstre bale,
Āmrā bali bānaprastha
Youbanetei bhālo cale.

Gharer madheye bakābaki,
Nānān mukhe nānān kathā.
Hājār loke najar paḍe,
Ekṭuku nāi biralatā.
Samay alpa, phurāy tāo
Arasiker ānāgonāy—
Ghantā dhare thāken tini
Satprasanga–ālocanāy.
Hatabhāgya nabīn yubā
Kājei thāke baner khoṁje,
Gharer madhye mukti ye nei
E kathā se biśeṣ bojhe.
Pancāśordhve bane yābe
Eman kathā śāstre bale,
Āmrā bali bānaprastha
Youbanetei bhālo cale.

Scripture Says

After fifty you'll go to the forest,
    So our scripture says
But we say a forest retreat is much
    Better in youthful days.
Bokuls flower in their plenty
    Koels sing unending,
Nature's arbours and vines are,
    Great for hiding and seeking.
Moonlight's play on *champak* branches
    Can't be mere illusion
Those who adore such things must have
    Under fifty's passion.
After fifty you'll go to the forest,
    So our scripture says
But we say a forest retreat is much
    Better in youthful days.

Inside the house all the lips are
    Busy with unending chatter;
Thousand eyes prying and poking,
    Privacy is a rare matter.
Time's so short. It is all wasted
    By the boring guests of course
Sitting down for hours
    Giving their holy discourse.
No wonder then that hapless youths
    Are forever seeking groves.
They know full well deliverance
    Is not to be found indoors.
After fifty you'll go to the forest,
    So our scripture says
But we say a forest retreat is much
    Better in youthful days.

Āmrā sabāi nabyakāler
　　Sabhya yubā anācārī,
Manur śāstra śudhre diye
　　Natun bidhi karba jari—
Buḍo thākun gharer koṇe,
　　Paysākaḍi karun jamā,
Dekhun base biṣay–patra,
　　Cālān māmlā–makaddamā,
Phagun–māse lagna dekhe
　　Yubārā jān baner pathe,
Rātri jege sādhyasādhan
　　Thākuk rata kaṭhin brate.
　Pancāśordhve bane yābe
　　Eman kathā śāstre bale,
　Āmrā bali bānaprastha
　　Youbanetei bhālo cale.

❄ ❄ ❄ ❄ ❄

We are young men of the present
    Age, modern and born to disobey.
Manu's old codes need amending
    We'll have new laws in our own way.
Let all old men stay at home and
    Pile up their rupees and pices,
Manage all affairs of the world,
    Litigate with legal advices.
Let the youth pick almanac-dates
    And in spring go to the forest
There let them do their desired things
    All night long without rest.
After fifty you'll go to the forest,
    So our scripture says
But we say a forest retreat is much
    Better in youthful days.

❄ ❄ ❄ ❄ ❄

Kalpanā, 1900

Yācanā

Bhalobese sakhī, nibhṛta yatane
  Āmār nāmṭi likhio— tomār
    Maner mandire.
Āmār parāne ye gān bājiche
  Tāhāri talṭi śikhio tomār
    Caranamanjīre.

Dhariā rākhio sohāge ādare
  Āmār mukhar pākhiṭi— tomār
    Prāsādaprānganẹ.
Mane kare sakhī, bāṁdhiā rākhio
  Āmār hāter rakhiṭi — tomār
    Kanakakakaṇkane.

Āmār latār ekṭi mukul
  Bhuliā tuliā rākhio—tomār
    Alakabandhane.
Āmār smaran śubha sindūre
  Ekṭi bindu āṁkio— tomār
    Lalāṭacandane.

Āmār manera mohera mādhuri
  Mākhiā rākhiā dio go— tomār
    Angasourabhe.
Āmār ākula jibana marana
  Ṭuṭiā luṭiā nio go— tomār
    Atula gourabe.

❄ ❄ ❄ ❄ ❄

Imagination, 1900

Entreaty

When you are all alone, my dear,
Do write my name with love and care
In the shrine of your memory sweet.
Teach the measure of the song
That buzzes in my soul
To the anklets round your feet.

There is my talking bird, take him
And bind him with your loving words
And keep in your mansion grand.
Remember to tie in a love-knot
The coloured thread round my wrist
To the gold bracelet on your hand.

Pluck a flower from my garden
In forgetfulness and place it
Carelessly in your tresses' braid.
Let my memory be the good
Omen vermilion beside
The sandal mark on your forehead.

Take the perfume of my passion
And let it be suffused with the
Fragrance pervading your being.
In your peerless splendour
Do snatch away and plunder
My troubled living and dying.

❄ ❄ ❄ ❄ ❄

Naibedya, 1901

No. 29

Krame mlān haye āse nayaner jyoti
Nayantārāy; bipulā e basumatī
Dhīre milāiyā āse chāyār matan
Laye tār sindhu śaila kāntār kānan.
Bicitra e biśvagān kṣin haye bāje
Indriyabīṇār sukṣma śatatantrī–mājhe;
Barṇe barṇe suranjita biśvacitrakhāni
Dhīre dhīre mṛdu haste lao tumi tāni
Sarbanga hṛday hate; dipta dipābali
Indriyer dvāre dvāre chila yā ujjvali
Dāo nibāiā; tār pare ardharāte
Ye nirmal mṛtyu sajyā pāta nijahāte
Se biśvabhubanhīn niḥśabda āsane
Ekā tumi basa āsi parama nirjane.

❄❄❄

No. 30

Bairāgya sādhane mukti, se āmār nay.

Asaṃkhya bandhan–mājhe mahānandamay
Labhiba muktir svād. Ei basudhār
Mrittikār pātrakhāni bhari bāraṃbār
Tomār amṛta dhāli dibe abirata
Nānābarṇa gandhamay. Pradīper mato
Samasta saṃsār mor lakṣa bartikāy
Jvālāye tulibe ālo tomāri śikhāy
Tomār mandir–mājhe.

Offerings to God, 1901

No. 29

Slowly the light turns nebulous
In my eyes. The earth enormous
With her oceans, mountains, meadows
And forests fade slow like shadows.
The diverse world-songs faintly echoes
In *veena* of fine nerve-strings of my senses.
You slowly gather with Your gentle hands
The world painted with many coloured bands
From my body and my mind. The blazing light
Which at my senses' doors were burning bright
You snuff them out, then halfway through the night
With your own hands you make a deathbed white.

You take your seat in that solitary place
Where the silent universe leaves no trace.

❄❄❄

No. 30

Salvation through negation I don't treasure.

Amidst countless bonds and unlimited pleasure
I will taste salvation. The clay cup
Of this earth again and again filling up
Will be pouring your ambrosia unending
In colours and fragrances. Like a lamp burning,
The world with my million wicks in flame
The illumination from your fire self–same
In your temple.

Indriyer dvār
Ruddha kari yogāsan, se nahe āmār.
Ya kichu ānanda āche dṛśye gandhe gāne
Tomār ānanda rabe tār mājhkhāne.

Moha mor mukti rupe uṭhibe jvaliā,
Prem mor bhakti rupe rahibe phaliā.

❄ ❄ ❄

No. 41

Taba pūjā nā ānile daṇḍa dibe tāre,
Yamadūt laye yābe naraker dvāre—
Bhaktihīne ei bali ye dekhāy bhay
Tomār ninduk se ye, bhakta kabhu nay.

Hey biśvabhubanarāj, e biśvabhubane
Āpanāre sab ceye rekhecha gopane
Āpan mahimā–mājhe. Tomār sṛṣtir
Kṣudra bālukanātuku, kṣnik śiśir
Tārāo tomār ceye pratykṣa ākāre
Dike dike ghosanā kariche āpanāre.

Yā–kichu tomār tāi āpanār bali
Ciradin e saṃsār caliyāche chali—
Tabu se corer courya paḍe nā to dharā

Āpanāre janaite nai taba tvarā.

❄ ❄ ❄

Closing all senses' doors
In meditation is not my course.
All the joys that there are in sights, songs and scents
In the midst of it all Your delight will be present.

My desires will light up as liberation
And my love will be fruitful as devotion.

❄❄❄

No. 41

Those who frighten the people with your fury
Are blasphemers and don't know your glory.
They claim you'll punish those who are irreverent
By casting them into hell's eternal torment.

Lord of the universe, in your domain
Most concealed, yourself ever remain
In your glory. The little grain of sand,
The evanescent dewdrop of this land,
Even they, more than you demonstrate
All around their own manifest state.

All that is yours as its own, so claiming
The creation has always been deceiving –
Yet it never has been caught this fraud of the fraudulent.

And you are in no hurry to make yourself evident.

❄❄❄

No. 60

Ekadā e bhārater kon banatale
Ke tumi mahān prāṇ, kī ānandabale
Uccāri uṭhile ucce, ' Śono biśvajan,
Śono amṛter putra yata debgan
Dibyadhāmbāsi, āmi jenechi tāṁhāre,
Mahānta puruṣ yini āṁdhārer pare
Jyotirmay. Tāre jene, tār pāne cāhi
Mṛtyure langhite pāra, anya path nāhi.'

Ārbār e bhārate ke dibe go āni
Se mahā ānandamantra, se udāttabāṇī
Sañjībanī, svarge martye sei mṛtunjay
Parama ghoṣanā, sei ekānta nirbhay
Ananta amṛtabārta.

re mṛta bhārat,
Śudhu sei ek āche, nāhi anya path.

❄❄❄

No. 70

Tomār nyer daṇḍa pratyeker kare
Arpaṇ karecha nije. Pratyeker pare
Diyecha śāsanbhār, hey rājādhirāj.
Se guru sammān taba se durūha kāj
Namiyā tomāre yena śirodharya kari
Sabinaye. Taba kārye yena nāhi ḍari
Kabhu kāre.

No. 60

Once in an Indian forest region
What great soul with great elation
Declared aloud, "Hear ye, hear ye,
O the children of immortality
And the gods in heaven, Him I have known
The Great One, beyond darkness who alone
Is effulgent. Knowing and seeing Him, I say,
You can conquer death and there is no other way."

To this *Bharat* who will once again bring
That mantra of bliss, that divine tidings'
Elixir to heaven and earth, the death-defying
Lofty declaration, the solitary unflinching
Message of immortality.

O dead *Bharat*, it does say
That is the one and only way, there is no other way.

❄ ❄ ❄

No. 70

Your sceptre of justice you've entrusted
To everyone. Each You have invested
With the burden of its rule, O King of kings.
That onerous honour, Your difficult bidding
May I shoulder humbly. May I never
Fear anyone in doing Your work ever.

Kṣmā yethā kṣīn durbalata,
Hey rudra, niṣṭhur yena hate pāri tathā
Tomār ādeśe. Yena rasanāy mama
Satyabākya jhali uṭhe kharakhaḍgasama
Tomār ingite. Yena rākhi taba mān
Tomār bicārasane laye nija sthān.
Anyāy ye kare ār anyāy ye sahe
Taba ghrinā yena tāre tṛnasama dahe.

❄ ❄ ❄ ❄ ❄

May I, O my Lord, can be severe
At Your command where mercy is mere
Weakness. May my speech truthful blaze
Like a sword's shimmering edge
At Your wish. Your standard may I meet
When I sit on Your judgement seat.
He who does inflict or condone inequity
May Your wrath burn them like straw, as both are guilty.

❄ ❄ ❄ ❄ ❄

Smaran, 1903

No. 2

Se yakhan beṁce chila go, takhan
Yā diyeche bārbār
Tār pratidān diba ye ekhan
Se samay nāhi ār.
Rajanī tāhār hayeche prabhāt,
Tumi tāre āji layecha hey nāth—
Tomāri caraṇe dilām saṁpiā
Kṛtjña upahār.

Tār kāche yata karechinu doṣ,
Yata gaṭechila truṭi,
Tomā–kāche tār māgi laba kṣamā
Caraṇer tale luṭi.
Tāre yāhā–kichu deyoā hay nāi,
Tāre yāhā–kichu saṁpibāre cāi,
Tomāri pujār thālāy dharinu
Āji se premer hār.

❄ ❄ ❄

No. 5

Āmār gharete ār nāi se ye nāi—
Yāi ār phire āsi, khuṁjiā nā pāi.
Āmār gharete nāth, eiṭuku sthan—
Sethā hate yā hārāy mele nā sandhān.
Ananta tomār gṛha, biśvamay dhām,
Hey nāth, khuṁjite tāre sethā āsilām.

Remembering, 1903

No. 2

Forever the time is gone
    Now to give in return
What she gave time and again
    While she was alive then.
Her night has turned to day,
    Oh Lord, You've taken her away,
At your feet my gratitude
    I offer You in reverence.

Whatever wrong I might have done
    And all my omission,
For all that I beg Your pardon
    At your feet in prostration.
Whatever I could not give her,
    Whatever I want to offer,
As a necklace of love
    I offer You in reverence.

❄ ❄ ❄

No. 5

In my home she is not anymore.
I come and go, find her no more.
O Lord, though small is my earthly place
Whatever I lose find no trace.
Your own realm is so vast,
I've come to seek her there at last.

Dāṁḍālem taba sandhyā–gaganer tale,
Cāhilām tomā–pane nayaner jale.
Kono mukh, kono sukh, āśātriṣā kono
Sethā hate hārāite pāre nā kakhono,
Sethāy enechi mor pīḍita e hiyā—
Dāo tāre, dāo tāre, dāo dubaiā.
Ghare ār nāhi mor ye amṛtaras
Biśva–mājhe pāi se hārāno paraś.

❄❄❄❄❄

I stand under the evening sky
And look at you with tearful eye.
From where can never be missing—
A face, joy, hope, or yearning.
I bring my heart in despair.
Please my Lord, drown, drown it there.
The nectar that is lacking in my home
I find its lost touch under Your world's dome .

❄ ❄ ❄ ❄ ❄

Śiśu, 1903

Samālocak

Bābā nāki bai lekhe sab nije.
Kichui bojhā yāy nā lekhen ki je.
Sedin paḍe śonacchilen tore,
Bujhechili?—bal mā satyi kare.
    Eman lekhāy tabe
    Bal dekhi ki habe.
Tor mukhe mā, yeman kathā śuni,
Teman kena lekhen nā ko uni.
Thakurmā ki bābāke kakṣano
Rājār kathā śonāy niko kono.
    Se–sab kathāguli
    Gechen bujhi bhuli?

Snān karte belā hala dekhe
Tumi kebal yāo mā, deke deke—
Khābār niye tumi basei thāko,
Se kathā tār manei thāke nāko.
    Karen sāra belā
    Lekhā–lekhā khelā

Bābār ghare āmi khelte gele
Tumi āmāy bala, 'duṣṭu chele'
Baka āmāy gol karle pare,
'Dekhchis ne likhchen bābā ghare
    Bal to satyi bal,
    Likhe ki hay phal.

The Child, 1903

Critic

Father writes books all by himself you say.
I don't understand what he writes anyway.
The other day when he read them to you,
Did you understand, Mother? Tell me true.
  Tell me, what good will come to us
  From all the writing that he does?
Why doesn't he write the way
About stories I hear you say?
Didn't grandma tell him ever
Stories about kings however?
    About those things I think
    He doesn't recall a wink.

When it is time for bath then
You call him again and again—
He doesn't seem to be aware
That with his food you are waiting there.
  With his writing all day long
  He keeps playing along.

When I go in his room to play
I am a naughty boy, you say.
You scold me if a little noise I'm making.
You say, "Can't you see that father is writing?"
    Tell me the truth of the thing,
    What good writing will bring?

Āmi yakhan bābār khātā tene
Likhi base doāt kalam ene—
Ka kha ga gha ṅ ha ya ba ra
Āmār belā kena mā rāg kara.
Bābā yakhan lekhe
Kathā kao nā dekhe.
Baḍo baḍo rul kaṭā kāgaj
Naṣṭa bābā karen na ki roj.
Āmi yadi nauko karte cāi
Amni balo, naṣṭa karte nāi.
Sādā kāgaj kālo
Karle bujhi bhālo?

❄ ❄ ❄

Rājār bāḍi

Āmār rājār bāḍi kothāy keu jāne nā se to
Se bāḍi ki thakto yadi loke jante peto.
Rupo diye deāl gāṁthā, sonā diye chāt,
Thāke thāke siḍi oṭhe sādā hatir dāt.
Sāt–mahalā koṭhāy sethā thāken suorāni,
Āmār rājār bāḍi kothāy śon mā, kāne kāne—
Chāder paśe tulsi gācher tab āche yeikhāne.

Rājkanyā ghumoy kothā sāt sāgarer pāre,
Āmi chāḍā ār keha to pāy nā khuṁje tāre.
Du hāte tār kāṁkan duṭi, dui kāne dui dul,
Khāṭer theke māṭir pare luṭiye paḍe cul.
Ghum bheṅe tār yābe yakhan sonār kaṭhi chuṁye
Hāsite tār manikguli paḍbe jhare bhuṁye.
Rājkanyā ghumoy kothā śon mā, kāne kāne—
Chāder paśe tulsi gācher tab āche yeikhāne.

When father's notebook I do sight,
And with his pen and ink I write
A b c d e f x y z
Why in my case you get cross with me?
    But when father is writing
    You just look and say nothing.
Pages after pages of ruled paper
Everyday he wastes forever!
If I want to make a paper boat ever
At once you say I must waste never.
    Is it good to turn white
    Papers into dark as night?

❄❄❄

King's Castle, Shishu

Where my king's castle is not known to any one.
It wouldn't be there if it were known to everyone.
The walls are made with silver and the roof is with solid gold
The stairs are stacked up like white elephant's tusks I am told.
In the seven-chamber mansion resides the pet-queen
Made with gems of seven kingdoms, her necklace has been.
I'll whisper to your ear, Mother, where is that king's castle
It is there on our roof where the potted *tulsis* dazzle.

On the shores of the seven seas the princess sleeps alone
Her address is known to; to others is unknown.
Two bangles on two wrists and two ear rings she only wears
From the bed to the floor below falls all her pretty hair.
With the touch of the gold rod she will wake forever
From her smile, to the floor all the gems will scatter.
I'll whisper to you, Mother, where the princess sleeps
It is there on our roof where the potted *tulsi* keeps.

Tomrā yakhan ghāṭe cala snāner belā hale
Āmi takhan cupi cupi yāi ye chāde cale.
Pāṁcil beye chāyākhāni paḍe mā, yei kone
Seikhānete pā chaḍiye basi āpan–mane.
Saṅge śudhu niye āsi mini beḍālṭāke,
Seo jāne nāpit bhāyā konkhānete thāke.
Jānis nāpitpāḍā kothāy? Śon mā, kāne kāne
Chāder paśe tulsi gācher tab āche yeikhāne.

❄❄❄❄❄

When you go to the pond for your daily bath
Then quietly I follow, Mother, our roof's path.
The shadow climbs the wall and in the corner it rests
I sit there absorbed in myself, stretching my two legs.
It's only the kitten that comes along with me.
Mother dear, he too knows where the barber can be
Do you know where the barber village is? I will whisper.
It is there on our roof where the potted *tulsi* flowers.

❄ ❄ ❄ ❄ ❄

Kheyā, 1906

Śeṣ kheyā

Diner śeṣe ghumer deśe ghomṭā–parā oi chāyā
Bhulālo re bhulālo mor prān.
O pārete sonār kule āṁdhārmule kon māyā
Geye gela kāj–bhānāno gān.
Nāmiye mukh cukiye sukh yābār mukhe yāy yārā
Pherār pathe phireo nāhi cāy,
Tāder pāne bhāṁṭār ṭāne yaba re āj gharchāḍā—
Sandhyā āse din ye cale yāy.
Ore āy
Āmāy niye yābi ke re
Dinaśeṣer śeṣ kheyāy.

Sāṁjher bela bhāṁtār srote o pār hate ekṭānā
Ekṭi duṭi yāy ye tari bhese.
Keman kare cinba ore oder mājhe konkhānā
Āmār ghāṭe chila āmār deśe.
Astācaler tīrer tale ghana gācher kol gheṁṣe
Chāyāy yena chāyār mato yāy,
Ḍākle āmi khanek thāmi hethāy pāḍi dharbe se
Eman neye āche re kon nāy.
Ore āy
Āmāy niye yabi ke re
Dinaśeṣer śeṣ kheyāy.

Gharei yārā yābār tārā kakhan geche gharpāne,
Pāre yārā yābār geche pāre;
Ghareo nahe, pāreo nahe, ye jan āche mājhkhāne
Sandhyābelā ke ḍeke ney tāre.

The Ferry, 1906

The Last Ferry

At the end of the day, a veiled shadow from the land of dreams
Beguiles me, steals my attention.
On the far bank, near the golden shore, a dim vision gleams
Singing of work-interruption.
With bowed heads, satisfied, those who go on before,
Don't even look back.
Leaving home with the ebb tide I'll go to that shore.
The day ends and comes eve black.
O you come to carry
Me in the last ferry.

From the other shore a boat or two steadily float
In the evening ebb tide.
How I shall recognise among them the very boat
Which was at my pier on this side?
Hugging the dense forest line in the setting sun's rays
Like shadows they fade into shadow.
In which boat is the boatman who will come my way
For a moment if I call him so.
O you come to carry
Me in the last ferry.

Those who were home bound have gone long before
Gone also are those bound for the shore
He who is neither home nor on shore but halfway
In this evening who will take him away?

Phuler bār nāi ko ār, phasal yār phalla nā—
Sei baseche ghāṭer kinārāy.
Ore āy
Āmāy niye yabi ke re
Dinaśeṣer śeṣ kheyāy.

❄ ❄ ❄

Duḥkhamurti

Duḥkher beśe esecha bale
Tomāre nāhi dariba hey.
Yekhāne byāthā tomāre sethā
Nibiḍ kare dhariba hey.
Āṁdhāre mukh dhākile svāmi,
Tomāre tabu ciniba āmi;
Maranrupe āsile prabhu,
Caran dhari mariba hey—
Yeman kare dāo nā dekhā
Tomāre nāhi dariba hey.

Nayane āji jhariche jal,
Jharuk jal nayane hey.
Bājiche buke, bājuk taba
Kaṭhin bāhubāṁdhane hey.
Tumi ye ācha bakse dhare
Bedanā tāhā jānāk more,
Cāba nā kichu kaba nā kathā
Cāhiyā raba badane hey.
Nayane āji jhariche jal,
Jharuk jal nayane hey.

❄ ❄ ❄ ❄ ❄

The one without flowers and has no harvest
Would rather laugh than shed a tear
When the day's light is gone and with lamp he is not blessed
Alone he waits on the pier.
O you come to carry
Me in day's last ferry.

❄❄❄

The Face of Grief

Because You've come as grief
I do not scare.
I will embrace You firmly
Where my pain is there.
Your face in the dark hidden it may be
Yet, my Lord, I will recognise thee.
You have come as death, my Lord
I'll die bowed at your feet.
I will not be afraid
In whatever form You greet.

Today my eyes are raining tears.
Let it rain.
Your hard arms' clasp wrenches my heart.
Let it pain.
To Your bosom You're holding me
Through my pain that fact I see.
I'll want nothing, say not a word
At Your face I'll gaze.
Today my eyes are raining tears
O let tears rain rage.

❄❄❄❄❄

Gitānjali, 1910

No. 8

Āj dhāner kṣete raudrachāyāy lukocurir khelā re bhāi, lukocurir khelā
Nīl ākāśe ke bhāsāle sādā megher bhelā re bhāi– lukocurir khelā.
Āj bhramar bhole madhu khete–uḍe beḍāy āloy mete,
Āj kiser tare nadīr care cakhacakhir melā.
Ore, jābonā āj ghare re bhāi, jābonā āj ghare.
Ore, ākāś bhene bahirke āj nebo re luṭ kare.
Yena joār–jale phenār rāśi batāse āj chuṭche hāsi
Āj binā kāje bājiye bāsi kāṭbe sakal belā.

***

Song Offering (1910)

No. 8

In the paddy field today the light and shadow are playing
hide and seek, O brother, playing hide and seek!
Who has floated white clouds' sail-boats in the blue sky?
O brother, it's a game of hide and seek!
Today the bees have forgotten to drink honey,
They just fly enchanted by the sky so sunny.
Why in the river-island the *Brahmini* ducks
Are meeting cheek to cheek?

O brother, today we won't go indoors, won't go indoors
We will break open the sky's vault and plunder the outdoors
As if on the ebb tide endless foam is floating
So with the wind, ceaseless laughter is flying
Today we will pass the whole day
Without any work and with flute playing.

❄ ❄ ❄

No. 20

Āji jharer rāte tomār abhisār
        Parān sakhā bandhu hey āmār.
    Ākas kāṁde hatāśasama nāi ye ghum nayane mama
    Duār khuli hey priyatama, cāi je bāre bār.
        Bāhire kichu dekhite nāhi pāi,
        Tomār patha kothāy bhābi tāi.
Sudur kon nadira pāre gahana kon banera dhāre
Gabhira kon andhakāre hatecha tumi pār.

❄ ❄ ❄

No. 44

    Jagate ānandayajñe āmār nimantraṇa.
        Dhanya hala, dhanya hala mānabajībana.
Nayan āmār rūper pure sādh miṭāye beḍāy ghure,
        Śraban āmār gabhīr sure hayeche magana.
        Tomār yajñe diyecha bhār, bajāi āmi bāṁśi —
        Gāne gāne geṁthe beḍāi prāner kānnā hāsi.
Ekhan samay hayeche ki? sabhāy giye tomāy dekhi
    Jayadvani śuniye jaba e mor nibedan.

❄ ❄ ❄

No. 20

In this stormy night
It is your love-tryst,
Soul mate mine,
Dear friend of mine.

The sky wails in distress
And my eyes are sleepless.
Opening my door, my darling,
Again and again I'm searching

I can't see anything outdoors.
I ponder where is the path of yours,
In which distant riverside,
In which dreary forest's side,
In darkness deepening,
How are you traversing?

❄ ❄ ❄

No. 44

My call is for the sacred rite of bliss on this earth.
Blessed I am and blessed too is this human-birth.
My sated eyes roam this world beautiful.
My ears are steeped in an air deeply tuneful.
At your command, playing my flute is my duty.
With songs I lace a lei of pain and gaiety.
Has the time come now? This is my only plea
    That in Your court I may cheer, "Victory to thee."

❄ ❄ ❄

No. 28

Prabhu, tomā lāgi āṁkhi jāge;
Dekhā nāi pāi
Patha cāi,
Seo mane bhālo lāge.
Dhulāte basiyā dvāre bhikhari hṛdaya hā re
Tomāri karunā māge;
Kripā nāi pāi
Sudhu cāi,
Seo mane bhālo lāge.
Āji e jagat mājhe kata sukhe kata kāje
Cale gela sabe āge;
Sāthi nāi pāi
Tomāy cāi,
Seo mane bhālo lāge.
Cāri dike sudhā–bharā bayākul śyāmal dharā
Kāṁdāy re anurāge;
Dekhā nāi pāi
Byāthā pāi,
Seo mane bhālo lāge.

❄ ❄ ❄

No. 60

Biśva yakhan nidrā magan, gagan andhakār,
Ke dey āmar bīnār tāre emana jhankār.
Nayane ghum nila keḍe, uṭhe basi śayan cheḍe —
Mele āṁkhi ceye thāki, pāi ne dekhā tār.

No. 28

Lord, for You my wakeful eyes are looking.
You, I don't face,
At the road I gaze,
To my mind that, too, is pleasing.
Sitting on the doorstep alert, alas, is this beggar-heart.
Your grace I don't get,
Only that's what I covet,
To my mind that, too, is pleasing.
Today amid this earth with endless work and mirth,
No comrades anymore,
All have gone before,
But You I'm wanting
To my mind that, too, is pleasing.
In the fervent green earth around with ambrosia it abounds
In devotion, ah, it sets me weeping.
Me, You forsake,
For You I ache,
To my mind that, too, is pleasing.

❄ ❄ ❄

No. 60

When the world is in sleep
And the sky is azure deep,
Who is that by His soft strumming
Sends my *veena*[1] in such a melody blazing?
With my eyes sleepless,
I leave my bed restless,
Open eyed I seek to greet
But Him I do not meet.

Guñjariā guñjariā prān uṭhila pure,
Jānine kon bipul bānī bāje byākul sure.
Kon bedanāy bujhi nā re hṛiday bharā aśrubhāre,
Pariye dite cāi kāhāre āpan kanṭha hār.

❄ ❄ ❄

No. 24

Yadi tomār dekhā nā pāi, prabhu, ebār e jībane
Tabe tomāy āmi pāi ni yena se kathā ray mane.
Yena bhule nā yāi, bedanā pāi śayane svapane.
E saṃsārer hāṭe
Āmār yatai dibas kāṭe,
Āmār yatai du hāt bhare uṭhe dhane
Tabu kichui āmi pāi ni yena se kathā ray mane.
Yena bhule nā yāi, bedanā pāi śayane svapane.
Yadi ālasbhare
Āmi basi pather 'pare
Yadi dhulāy sayan pāti sayatane,
Yena sakal pathi āche bāki se kathā ray mane
Yena bhule nā yāi, bedanā pāi śayane svapane.
Yatai uṭhe hāsi,
Ghare yatai bāje bāṁśi,
Ogo yatai gṛha sājai āojane,
Yena tomāy ghare hayani ānā se kathā ray mane.
Yena bhule nā ŷāi, bedanā pāi śayane svapane.

❄ ❄ ❄ ❄ ❄

Slowly a song's murmur fills my being
With a titanic message in yearning—
I don't know what feeling doleful
Fills my being and makes eyes tearful.
Around whose neck I want to place,
I know not, my jewelled necklace.

❄ ❄ ❄

No. 24

If, my Lord, in this life I do not have your greeting,
That I didn't have your vision let my mind be remembering.
May I have pain in sleep and dream lest I should be forgetting.
In the world's marketplace,
The more I pass my days,
The more riches, with my two hands, I keep gathering
Let me keep in mind that I have nothing.
May I have pain in sleep and dream lest I should be forgetting.
If in me sloth does abide,
On the wayside I do reside,
If with care on the dust I spread my bedding.
That I'm yet to walk most of the path let my mind be remembering
May I have pain in sleep and dream lest I should be forgetting
The more laughter surges on,
The more the flute plays upon,
The more my room, O dear, I may be beautifying,
That I didn't bring You in it, my mind be remembering.
May I have pain in sleep and dream lest I should be forgetting.

❄ ❄ ❄ ❄ ❄

Gitimālya 1914

No. 40

Jāni go, din yābe e din yābe.
Ekadā kon belāśeṣe malin rabi karun hese
Śeṣ bidāyer cāoā āmār mukher pāne cābe.
Pather dhāre bājbe benu, nadīr kule carbe dhenu,
Āṅgināte khelbe śiśu, pakhirā gān gābe —
Tabuo din yābe e din yābe.
Tomār kāche āmār e minati
Yābār āge jāni yena āmāy ḍekechila kena
Ākāś pāne nayan tule śyāmal basumatī.

Kena niśār nirabatā śuniye chila tārār kathā,
Parāne ḍheu tulechila kena diner jyoti —
Tomār kāche āmār ei minati.
Sāṅga ŷabe habe dharār pālā
Yena āmār gāner śeṣe thāmte pāri śame ese —
Chayṭi ṛitur phule phale bharte pāri dālā.
Ei jībaner ālokete pāri tomāy dekhe yete
Paḍiye yete pāri tomāy āmār galār māla —
Saṅga yabe habe dharār pālā.

❄❄❄

Garland of Songs, 1914

No. 40

I know this day too shall pass.
At the end of one day, alas,
The setting sun will bid goodbye
With its last sad smile on my eye.
The flute will play on the wayside,
Cows will graze by the riverside,
Children will play on the courtyard-grass
Birds will sing and this day too shall pass.
This is my plea to Thee: before I go
May I know why did the green earth below
With her eyes to the sky call me so?

Why did the silence of the night
Say the words of the stars so bright?
Why the day's radiance so danced in my heart?
These answers, Lord, I beg of Thee impart.
When my earthly role will end, oh let me
End my song on beat and quite on key.
May the fruits and flowers of the field
Of the six seasons to my basket yield.
With the light of this life may I see
That I can place my garland on Thee
Before my earthly role's end shall be.

❄ ❄ ❄

No. 26

Peyechi chuṭi bidāy deha bhāi —
Sabāre āmi pranām kare yāi.
Phirāye dinu dvārer cābi, rākhi nā ār gharer dābi —
Sabār āji prasādabāṇī cāi.
Anek din chilām pratibeśī,
Diyechi yata niyechi tār beśi.
Prabhat haye eseche rāti, nibiyā gela koṇer bāti —
Pareche ḍāk, calechi āmi tāi.

* * *

No. 67

Ye rāte mor duāraguli bhāṅla jhaḍe
Jāni nāi to tumi ele āmār ghare.
Sab ye haye gela kālo, nibe gelo dīper ālo,
Ākāś pāne hāt bāḍālem kāhāra tare?
Andhakāre rainu paḍe svapana māni.
Jhaḍ ye tomār jayadhvajā tāi ki jāni.
Sakāl bela ceye dekhi, dāṁḍiye ācho tumi e ki
Ghar–bharā mor śūnyatāri bukera 'pare.

* * * * *

No. 26

I've got my leave, O brother, bid me adieu.
I depart with my salutes to all of you.
        I returned the key to the room,
        No more claim to it I presume.
Only the message of peace I seek from you.
        I lived for long as your neighbour,
        I received more than I did offer.
        The night is about to dawn,
        The light in the corner is gone,
My call's here, so with adieu I take leave of you.

❄ ❄ ❄

No. 67

I didn't know that You came to my shore
When the stormy night broke down my door.
The lamp went out and my world was in darkness.
For whom did I raise my hands to the sky limitless?
In darkness I did stay, thinking I was dreaming,
Didn't know the storm was your victory-banner flying.
In the morning, in awe, I did see You standing
Upon the emptiness of my home and my being.

❄ ❄ ❄ ❄ ❄

Gitāli, 1914

No. 1

Rātri ese yethāy meśe diner pārābāre
Tomāy āmāy dekhā hala sei mohānār dhāre.
Seikhānete sādāy kāloy mile geche āṁdhār āloy —
Seikhānete dheu chuṭeche e pāre oi pāre.

Nitalanīl nīraba–mājhe bājla gabhīr bānī,
Nikaṣete uṭhla phuṭe sonār rekhākhāni.
Mukher pāne tākāte yāi, dekhi–dekhi dekhte nā pāi —
Svapana–sāthe jaḍiye jāgā, kāṁdi ākul dhāre.

* * *

No. 14

Āmār sakal raser dhārā
Tomāte āj hok–nā hārā.
Jīban juḍe lāguk paras, bhuban byepe jāguk haraṣ,
Tomār rūpe maruk dube āmār duṭi āṁkhitārā.
Hāriye yāoā manti āmār
Phiriye tumi ānle ābār.
Chariye paḍā āśāguli kuḍiye tumi lao go tuli,
Galār hāre dolāo tāre gāṁthā tomār kare sārā.

* * *

Harvest of Songs, 1914

No. 1

Where on the day's seashore the night does meet,
It was near the same inlet that we did greet.
        There amid the darkness and light
        Is the unison of black and white.
Waves roll there from shore to shore in delight.

From the deep blue silence came the poignant message.
From the darkness did rise the golden line's image.
        Of the face I want to have a gleam,
        I almost see but it remains unseen.
I weep raining tears for waking up in the midst of dream.

❄ ❄ ❄

No. 14

Let all the feelings in me
On this day be lost in Thee.
        Let Your touch be there all through my life,
        All over the earth let delight thrive.
Let the light of my eyes drown in thy splendour.
You have brought back
My mind that had lost its track.
        O please gather
        All the hopes that I scatter,
Swing them from Your neck when Your weaving is over.

❄ ❄ ❄

No. 57

Tomār duār kholār dhvani oi go bāje hṛiday mājhe.
Tomār ghare niśi–bhore āgal yadi gela sare
Āmār ghare raiba tabe kiser lāje?
Anek balā balechi, se mithyā balā.
Anek calā calechi, se mithyā calā.
Āj yena sab pather śeṣe tomār dvāre dāḍāi ese —
Bhuliye yena ney nā more āpan kāje.

❄❄❄

No. 65

Megh baleche ' yāba yāba,' rāt baleche ' yāi',
Sāgar bale ' kūl mileche– āmi to ār nāi'.
Duḥkha bale ' rainu cupe tāhār pāyer cinha rupe',
Āmi bale 'milāi āmi ār kichu nā cāi'.
Bhuban bale ' tomār tare āche baranamālā',
Gagan bale ' tomar tare lakṣa pradip jvālā'.
Prem bale ye ' yuge yuge tomar lāgi āchi jege',
Maran bale ' āmi tomār jiban tarī bāi'.

❄❄❄❄❄

No. 57

In my heart the sound of Your door-opening came.
If the bar of Your room is opened
At dawn at the night's end
In my room shall I remain in what shame?
Much I have said, lies they are all.
Much I have travelled, vain they are all.
Today at the end of all the trails,
Let me stop here at Your door step.
Let not my work make me forget the debt.

❄ ❄ ❄

No. 65

'Go, I shall go,' says the cloud. The night says, 'I must leave,'
The sea says, 'I am no more for my shore I retrieve,'
'Like a sign of His feet', sorrow says, 'silent let me remain',
I say, 'Let me be in unison, I've nothing more to gain',
The world says, 'For You is the garland of reception',
'For You', says the sky, 'are lighted lamps a-million',
Love says, 'For You I remain awake through ages'.
'I ply Your vessel of life', Death announces.

❄ ❄ ❄ ❄ ❄

Utsarga, 1914

No.8

Āmi cañcala hey,
Āmi sudurera piāsī.
Din cale yāy, āmi ānmane
Tāri āśā ceye thāki bātāyane,
Ogo prāṇe mane āmi ye tāhār
Paraśa pābār prayāsī.
Āmi sudurera piāsī.
Ogo sudur, bipula sudūr, tumi ye
Bājāo byākula bāṁśari.
Mor ḍānā nāi, āchi ek ṭhāṁi,
Se kathā ye yāi pāsari.

Āmi utsuka hey,
Hey sudur, āmi prabāsī.
Tumi durlav durāśār mato
Ki kathā āmāy śunāo satata.
Taba bhāṣa śune tomāre hṛday
Jeneche tāhār svabhāsī.
Hey sudur, āmi prabāsī.
Ogo sudur, bipula sudūr, tumi ye
Bājāo byākula bāṁśari.
Nāhi jāni path, nāhi mor rath
Se kathā ye yāi pāsari.

Dedications, 1914

No. 8

Restless am I,
Longing for faraway.
Days fly, I look for it hopefully,
Through the window absent–mindedly
With my heart and soul.
I am eager for its touch.
I seek the distant so much
Oh odyssey, the vast odyssey
In your flute an ardent tune you play.
I forget that I have no wings
And in the same place I stay.

Oh I am craving.
O distant I am in a foreign land.
Like an unattainable longing,
Always some message you're sending.
Hearing your message, my heart
Feels a kinship with you.
O faraway I am in a foreign land.
Oh odyssey, the vast odyssey
In your flute an ardent tune you play.
I forget that I have no chariot
And I don't know the way.

Āmi unmanā hey,
Hey sudūr, āmi udāsī.
Roudra–mākhāno alasa belāy
Taru marmare chāyār khelāy,
Ki murati taba nilākāśśāyī
Nayane uṭhe go abhāsi.
Hey sudūr, āmi udāsī.
Ogo sudūr, bipula sudūr, tumi ye
Bājāo byākula bāṁśari.
Kakṣe āmār ruddha duār
Se kathā ye yāi pāsari.

❄ ❄ ❄

No. 17

Dhūp āpanāre milāite cāhe gandhe,
Gandha se cāhe dhūpere rahite juḍe.
Sur āpanāre dharā dite cāhe chande,
Chanda phiriyā chuṭe yete cāhe sure.
Bhāb pete cāy ruper mājhāre anga,
Rūp pete cāy bhāber mājhāre chāḍā.
Asīm se cāhe simār nibiḍ sanga,
Sīmā pete cāy asīmer mājhe hārā.
Pralaye srijane nā jāni e kāhār yukti,
Bhāb hate rupe abirām yāoā āsā,
Bandha phiriche khuṁjiā āpan mukti,
Mukti māgiche bāṁdhaner mājhe bāsā.

❄ ❄ ❄ ❄ ❄

Absent minded I am.
O distant, detached I am,
In the sun-drenched idle day
In the tree murmurs and shadows' play
When a glimpse of your sight in the blue sky
Unfolds before my eyes
O distant, detached I am.
Oh odyssey, the vast odyssey
In your flute an ardent tune you play.
I forget that I have no wings
And in the same place I stay.

❄❄❄

No. 17

The incense longs to unite with the fragrance.
The fragrance longs to melt into the incense.
The tune yearns to be attached to the cadence.
The cadence yearns to return to the tune's essence.
The spirit ever wants the form's delight.
The form wants to lose itself in the spirit.
The infinite aches to melt in the finite.
The finite aches to fade in the infinite's presence.
Don't know whose logic is destruction and creation.
Constant is spirit and form's exchange.
The search of bondage for its own salvation
And salvation's quest for nest in bondage.

❄❄❄❄❄

Balākā, 1916

No. 19

Āmi ye besechi bhālo ei jagatere;
Pāke pāke phere phere
Āmār jiban diye jaḍyechi ere;
Prabhāt–sandhyār
Ālo–andhakār
Mor cetanāy geche bhese;
Ābaśeṣe
Ek haye geche āj āmār jīban
Ār āmār bhuban.
Bhālobāsiyāchi ei jagater ālo
Jībanere tāi bāsi bhālo.

Tabuo marite habe eo satya jāni.
Mor bāṇi
Ekdin e–bātāse phuṭibe nā,
Mor āṁkhi e–āloke luṭibe nā,
Mor hiayā chuṭibe nā
Āruner uddipta āhbāne;
Mor kāne kāne
Rajanī kabe nā tār rahasyabāratā,
Śeṣ kare yete habe śeṣ dṛṣti, mor śeṣ kathā.

Eman ekānta kare cāoā
Eo satya yata
Eman ekānta cheḍe yāoā
Seo sei mato.
E duer mājhe tabu konokhāne āche kono mil
Nahile nikhil

Wild Geese, 1914

No. 19

I have loved this world dearly.
With my life truly
I've draped it around thoroughly.
Morning and dusk
Light and shadow's mask
Wafted in my consciousness.
Merged into oneness
At long last
My life and the world so vast.
The light of this world I adore
My life I love therefore.

Yet I must die, I know it to be true.
My message too
One day in the wind it won't be.
This feast of light my eyes won't see.
My heart will not run at all
With the resplendent dawn's call.
In whispers
To my ears
The night will not reveal her secret presage
End will come to my last look, my last message.

This earnest yearning
As true it is
This certain farewell
So too it is.
Amidst these two there is somewhere unity.
Or this universe with certainty

Etabaḍo prabaṇcanā
Hāsimukhe etakāl kichute bahite pārita nā.
Sab tār ālo
Kīṭe–kāṭā puṣpasama etadine haye yeta kālo.

***

No. 28

Pākhire diyecha gān, gāy sei gān,
Tār beśi kare nā se dān.
Āmāre diyecha svar, āmi tār beśi kari dān,
Āmi gāi gān.

Bātāsere karecha svādhīn,
Sahaje se bhṛtya taba bandhanbihīn.
Āmāre diyecha yata bojhā,
Tāi niye cali pathe kabhu bāṁkā kabhu sojā.
Eke eke phele bhār marane marane
Niye yāi tomār carane
Ekdin riktahasta sebāy svādhīn;
Bandhan yā dile more kari tāre muktite bilīn.

Purnimāre dile hāsi;
Sukhasvapna–rasarāśi
Dhale tāi, dharaṇīr karaput sudhāy ucchvasi.
Duḥkhakhāni dile mor tapta bhāle thuye,
Āśrujale tāre dhuye dhuye
Ananda kariyā tāre phirāye āniyā dei hāte
Dinaśeṣe milaner rāte.

Tumi to gaḍecha sudhu e māṭir dharani tomār
Milāiyā āloke āṁdhār.

Could not bear with smile
For so long this splendid guile.
By now all her light
Would have turned black like a flower with insects' blight.

❄❄❄

No. 28

You gave birds the gift of song and they sing,
Further they give nothing.
You granted me voice but I give more
Songs from it, I pour.

You gave the air freedom's advantage.
Easily it is your slave, without bondage.
All the loads You gave me
I carry them on my way, winding or straight as it may be.
In death after death the loads I shed one by one.
At Your feet I run
To serve you with empty hands, as the bondage you dealt
In freedom it had melt.

To the full moon You gave a face smiling.
So with sweetness overflowing
It fills the earth with joy and happy dreams unending.
For my fate You have allotted pain
With tears I wash again and again
To bring them to You as joy at night
When the day ends and we unite.

You have made only this earth of clay
With darkness and light's play.

Śūnyahāte sethā more rekhe
Hāsicha āpani sei śunyer āḍāle gupta theke.
Diyecha āmār pare bhār
Tomār svargaṭi racibār.

Ār sakalere tumi dāo,
Śudhu mor kāche tumi cāo.
Āmi yāhā dite pāri āpanār preme,
Siṃhāsan hate neme
Hasimukhe bakse tule nāo.
Mor hāte yāhā dāo
Tomār āpan hāte tār beśi phire pāo tumi.

***

No. 37

Dūr hate ki śunis mṛtyur garjan, ore din
Ore udāsin,
Oi krandaner kalarol,
Lakṣa bakṣa hate mukta rakter kallol.
Bahnibanyā–taraṅger beg,
Biṣaśvās–jhaṭikār megh,
Bhutal gagan
Murchita bihval–karā maraṇe maraṇe āliṅgan;
Ori mājhe path cire cire
Nūtan samudratīre
Tarī niye dite habe pāḍi,
Dākiche kāndārī
Eseche ādeś—
Bandare bandhan kāl ebārer mato hala śes,
Purāno sañcay niye phire phire becākenā
Ār calibe nā.

Leaving me empty handed here
Cloaked behind the emptiness You smile there.
To me You have given
The task of fashioning Your heaven.

To all the others You give
Only from me You want to receive.
Stepping down from Your throne
Keep in your heart with Your smiling face shown
What I can give you with love and ardour.
You get back in your own hands more
Than that in my hands you pour.

❄ ❄ ❄

No. 37

From a distance do you hear the thunder of death, o you indigent,
O you indifferent,
The din of wailing,
The clamour of blood from a million hearts gushing?
The current of volcanic rage surging,
Clouds of poisoned breath swelling
Make the heaven and earth faint, bewilder,
And clasp one death after another.
Surmounting all, a way must be found
For the boat to be onward bound
For a new ocean shore,
For the helmsman's call soars—
Command is clear.
Stagnant time in the port must end here.
Buying and selling with past saving therefore
Can't go on anymore.

Bañcanā bāḍiya oṭhe, phurāy satyer yata puṁji,
Kāṇḍāri dākiche tāi bujhi—
"Tuphāner majhkhāne
Nūtan samudratīrpāne
Dite habe pāḍi."
Tāḍatāḍi
Tāi ghar chaḍi
Cāridik hate oi dāmḍ–hāte chuṭe āse dāḍi.

'Nūtan uṣār svarṇadvār
Khulite bilamba kata ār.'
E kathā śudhāy sabe
Bhīta ārtarabe
Ghum hate akasmāt jege.
Jhaḍer puñjita meghe
Kāloy dhekeche ālo—jāne nā to keu
Rātri āche ki nā āche, digante phenāye uṭhe dheu—
Tāri mājhe phukāre kāṇḍārī—
"'Nūtan samudratīre tarī niye dite habe pāḍi."
Bāhiriyā ela kārā. Mā kāṁdiche piche,
Preyasī dāṁḍāye dvāre nayan mudiche.
Jhaḍer garjan mājhe
Biccheder hāhākār bāje;
Ghare ghare śunya hala ārāmer śajyātal;
"Yātrā karo yātra karo yātrīdal,"
Uṭhiche ādeś,
"Bandarer kāl hala śeṣ."

Mṛtyu bhed kari
Duliyā caleche tarī.
Kothāy pouṁchibe ghāṭe, kabe habe pār,
Samay to nāi śudhābār.

Deceit is on the rise, drained is truth's capital,
That may be the reason for helmsman's call—
"In the midst of stormy waves' rage
You must voyage
To a new ocean shore."
Hastily therefore,
Leaving homes beforehand
Come running from all corners, oarsmen, with oars in hand.

"How long must we wait
For the opening of the new dawn's golden gate?"
Suddenly waking up from sleep
In frightened voices deep
This question all lips utter.
The storm clouds gather.
Darkness covers the light — it is not known
If it is still night. On the horizon waves rise on foam —
In their midst the helmsman voice does roar—
"With your boat you must voyage to a new ocean shore."
Many come out. Behind, a mother cries,
At the door a beloved shuts her eyes.
In the midst of roaring gale
Is heard separation's wail;
In home after home beds of comfort are bare.
"Voyageurs, start your journey, you must start then and there,"
Command is clear,
"Time in port must end here."

Death conquering
Pushes on the boat, rocking.
There is no time to demand
Where journey ends or where is the land?
Only this they know:
Rowing the boat they must go,

Ei śudhu jāniyāche sār
Taranger sāthe laḍi
Bahiyā calite habe tarī.
Eseche ādeś—
Bandarer kāl hala śeṣ.

Ajānā samudra tīr, ajānā se deś—
Sethākār lāgi
Uṭhiāche jāgi
Jhaṭikār kanṭhe kanṭhe śunye śunye pracaṇḍa āhvān.
Maraner gān
Uṭheche dhvaniā pathe nabajībaner abhisāre
Ghor andhakāre.
Yata duḥkha prithibīr, yata pāp, yata amaṅgal,
Yata aśrujal,
Yata hiṃsa halāhal
Samasta uṭhiche tarangiā,
Kul ullaṅghiā,
Ūrdha ākāśere byaṅgakari.
Tabu beye tarī
Sab ṭhele hate habe pār,
Kāne niye nikhiler hāhākār,
Śire laye unmatta durdin,
Citte niye āśā antahīn,
Hey nirbhīk, duḥkha–abhihata.
Ore bhāi, kār ninda kara tumi. Māthā kara nata.
E āmār e tomār pāp.
Bidhātār bakṣe ei tāp
Bahu yug hate jami bāyukone ājike ghanāy—
Bhīrur bhīrutāpuñja, prabaler uddhata anyāy,
Lobhīr niṣṭhur lobh,

Fighting the waves' onslaught,
With the sails taut,
Hand on helm steadfast,
Survive or die at last.
You must press on.
The boat must sail on.
Command is clear,
Time in port must end here.

Unknown is the seashore, unknown is the land,
For that place
From the empty space,
Sounds a fierce call in the roaring gale.
A death song's wail
At the quest for a new life does sound
In darkness profound.
All sorrows of the world, sins, evil's pain—
All tears rain,
All violence, all venom
Rise as waves fearsome,
Flooding the shore,
Mocking the sky o'er.
Even so, all surmounting
Must keep on rowing
And the boat must traverse.
In the ear will ring the cry of the universe.
O you sorrowful, stricken, fearless,
Fill your heart with hope endless.
Bear the weight of hard days' dread.
Brother mine, who do you blame? Bow your head.
It is mine, it is your transgression that rages.
The agony piled in the heart of God for ages
Gathers now in the corner of the sky.
The cowardice of all cowards, arrogant injustice of the high,
Cruel avarice of the greedy,

Bañciter nitya cittakṣobh,
Jāti abhimān,
Mānaber adhiṣṭhātr̄i debatār bahu asammān,
Bidhātār bakṣa āji bidāriyā
Jhaṭikār dirghaśvāse jale sthale beḍāy phiriā.
Bhaṅgiā paḍuk jhar, jāguk tuphān,
Niḥśeṣ haiyā jāk nikhiler yata bajrabān.
Rākho nindābāni, rākho āpan sādhutva–abhimān,
Śudhu ekmane hao pār
E pralay pārābār
Nūtan sṛṣṭir upakule
Nūtan bijaydhvajā tule.

Duḥkhere dekhechi nitya, pāpere dekhechi nānā chale;
Aśāntir ghūrni dekhi j̄ibaner srote pale pale;
Mṛtyu kare lukācuri
Samasta prithib̄i juḍi.
Bhese yāy tārā sare yāy
J̄ibanere kare yāy
Kṣanik bidrūp.
Āj dekho tāhāder abhrabhed̄i birāt svarūp.
Tār pare dāṁḍāo sammukhe,
Balo akampita buke—
"Tore nāhi kari bhay,
E–saṁsāre pratidin tore kariāchi jay.
Tor ceye āmi satya e–bisvāse prāṇ diba, dekh.
Śānti satya, śib satya, satya sei cirantan ek."

Mṛtyur antare paśi amrita nā pāi yadi khuṁje,
Satya yadi nāhi mele duḥkha sāthe jujhe,
Pāp yadi nāhi mare yāy
Āpanār prakāś–lajjāy,
Ahaṁkar bheṅe nāhi paḍe āpanār asahya sajjāy,

Desperation of the needy,
High castes' vanity blind,
And many insults to the presiding god of mankind,
Breaking out of God's breast
Swirl over land and sea like the long drawn sigh of a tempest.
Let the storm burst open, waves rage without end.
Let all thunders and other arms of the world spend.
Stop blaming others,
And vanity of piety's fare.
Single-mindedly press on,
Cross over this ocean of destruction
To a new beginning nigh
Holding the new victory banner high.

I've seen sorrow everyday and the evil in its many faces.
The whirlpools of conflict I've seen often in life's passage.
All over the world death plays the trick
With its game of hide and seek.
For a moment
They deride life's torment
And are then swept away, vanishing nigh.
Look at its real grotesque form piercing the sky.
Standing face to face,
Declare without fear's trace,
" I'm not afraid of you,
Everyday in my life I've vanquished you,
I'm truer than you. With this faith I'll sacrifice my life, I profess.
Peace is truth, auspicious is truth, truth is one and timeless."

Diving into the heart of death in search of the eternal, if I fail,
If I can't find the truth in my battles with travail,
If sin does not die from the shame of its disclosure,
Pride does not fall because of its intolerable pomp and grandeur,

Tabe ghar chāḍā sabe
Antarer ki āśvās–rabe
Marite chuṭeche śata śata
Prabhāter ālor pāne lakṣa lakṣa nakṣatrer mato.
Birer e raktasrot, mātār e aśrudhārā
Er yata mulya se ki dharār dhulay habe hārā.
Svarga ki habe nā kenā.
Bisver bhāndāri śudhibe na
Eta ṛṇ?
Rātrir tapasyā se ki ānibe nā din.
Nidāruṇ duḥkharāte
Mṛtyughāte
Manuṣ curṇila yabe nija martyasimā
Takhan dibe nā dekhā debatār amar mahimā.

❄ ❄ ❄ ❄ ❄

Then what solace can there be remaining
In the hearts of those who came out running?
Hundreds are rushing to embrace death aright
Like millions of stars running to the dawn's light.
The cost of the braves' blood, mothers' tears rain
Will they be lost in the dusts of the earth in vain?
Will not paradise be won?
Will not payment for all the debts be done
By the keeper of the world's treasure?
Will not the quest through the night usher
A new dawn?
In the night of untold affliction,
At death's invitation,
When man shattered his mortal limit
Would not then be seen the infinite glory's summit?

❄ ❄ ❄ ❄ ❄

Palātakā, 1918

Palātakā

Oi yekhāne śiri̅ṣ gāche
Jhuru–jhuru kaci pātār nāce
Ghāser pare chāyākhāni kāṁpāy tharathara
Jharā phuler gandhe bharabhara—
Oikhāne mor poṣā harin carta āpan mane
Henā beḍār kone
Śiter rode sārā sakālbelā.
Tāri saṅge karta khelā
Pāhāḍ theke ānā
Ghana raṅā roāy dhākā ekṭi kukurchānā.
Yena tārā dui bideśer duṭi chele
Mileche ek pāṭhśālāte, eksāthe tāi beḍāy hese khele.
Hāṭer dine pather kata loke
Beḍār kāche dāṁḍiye yeta, dekhta abāk cokhe.

Phāgun māse jagla pāgal dakhin hāoā,
Śiure oṭhe ākāś yena kon premiker raṅin–ciṭhi pāoā
Śāler bane phuler mātan hala śuru
Pātāy pātāy ghāse ghāse lāgla kāṁpan duruduru.
Harin ye kār udās–karā bāṇi̅
Haṭhāt kakhan śunte pele āmrā ki tā jāni.
Tāi ye kālo cokher kone
Cāuni tāhār utal hala akāraṇe;

Tāi se theke theke
Haṭhat āpan chāyā dekhe
Camke dāṁḍāy beṁke.

The Runaway, 1918

The Runaway

Where on the rain-tree yonder
In gentle breeze dance the leaves tender
And their shadows tingle on the grass below
The air currents, laden with perfume of fallen flower, flow—
It is there, where the *henna*-fence has grown
That my pet deer used to graze on its own.
Fetched from the hills a pup with deep red fur coat
Played with him in the morning sun in winter and dote,
As if two boys from two lands far away
Met in a kindergarten and spent time in laughter and play
On the market day many would stop by the fence
And watch them with surprise intense.

In *Phalgun* came the wild south wind, the sky felt a shiver
Of receiving a love letter from a lover.
Flowerfest began in the *shal* tree stand
Gentle throb ran through the leaves and grassland.
We had no inference
When the deer got, from whom, the message of indifference.
The look in his dark eyes so wonderful
For no reason became fretful.

That's why at the sight
Of his shadow he stared in fitful plight.

Ekadā ek bikālbelāy
Āmlakiban adhir yakhan jhikimiki ālor khelāy,
Tapta hāoā bythiye oṭhe āmer boler bāse,
Māṭher pare māṭh haye pār chuṭla harin niruddeśer āśe.
Sammukhe tār jībanmaran sakal ekākār,
Ajāniter bhay kichu nei ār.

Bhebechilām āṁdhār hale pare
Phirbe ghare
Cenā hāter ādar pābār tare.
Kukurchānā bāre bāre ese
Kāche gheṁse gheṁse
Keṁde–keṁde cokher cāoyāy ṣudhāy jane jane,
"Kothāy gela, kothāy gela, kena tāre nā dekhi aṅgane."
Āhār tyeje beḍāy se ye, ela nā tār sāthī.
Āṁdhār hala jalla gharer bāti;
Uṭhla tārā; māṭhe–māṭhe nāmla nīrab rāti.
Ātur cokher praśna niye phere kukur bāire ghare,
"Nāi se kena, yāy kena se kāhār tare."

Kena ye tā se–i ki jāne. Geche se yār ḍāke
Kono kāle dekhe nāi ye tāke.
Ākāś hate, ālok hate, natun pātār kāṁcā sabuj hate
Diśāhārā dakhin hāoār srote
Rakte tāhār keman elomelo
Kiser khabar ela.
Buke ye tār bājla bāṁśi bahuyuger phāgun–diner sure—
Kothāy anek dure
Rayeche tār āpan ceye āro āpan jan.
Tāri anneṣan.
Janma hate āche yena marme tāri lege,
Āche yena chuṭe calār bege,
Āche yena cala–capal cokher kone jege.

On one afternoon bright
When the *amlaki* stand was excited at the play of shimmering light,
The warm air was heavy with mango blossoms' scent
Crossing the fields and seeking the unknown the deer went.
Life or death became one of their own
And he had no fear of the unknown.

I thought he would come back
After it was dark
For known hands' loving touch.
The puppy, much too much,
Went hither thither
With tearful eyes seem to ask one after another
"Where can he be? Where did he go? Why isn't he in the court
yard, I can't discern?"
Forsaking his food he roamed around, but his playmate did
not return.
Darkness fell; in the house lamps gave light.
Stars came out; on the fields fell the silent night.
With questions in his anxious eyes the pup went in and out,
"Why isn't he here, for someone else why does he roam about?"

The deer too doesn't know why it is so. He has never seen her
Whose call he had to answer.
A desultory message came in his blood
From the sky, from the light, from the green of tender leaves' buds,
In the south wind that lost its way.
In his heart the age-old tune of spring a flute did play.
Far away, somewhere
There was someone dearer
Than his own self. For her he was searching.
She seemed to be in his heart from the beginning
All his running was for her sake
In his restless eyes she was awake.

Kono kāle cene nāi se yāre
Sei to tāhār cenāsonār khelādhulā ghocāy ekebāre.
Aṁdhār tāre ḍāk diyeche keṁde,
Ālok tāre rākhla nā ār beṁdhe.

❄ ❄ ❄

Śeṣ pratiiṣthā

Ei kathā sadā śuni, "geche cale", "geche cale."
Tabu rākhi bale
Balo nā, "se nāi."
Se–kathāṭā mithyā, tāi
Kichutei sahe nā ye,
Marme giye bāje.

Mānuṣer kāche
Yāoā–āsā bhāg haye āche.
Tāi tār bhāṣā
Bahe śudhu adhkhānā āśā.
Āmi cāi seikhāne milāite prān
Ye–samudre āche nāi pūrṇa haye rayeche samān.

❄ ❄ ❄ ❄ ❄

She who has always been unknown
Has ended for good all his playing with the known.
He had heard the call of darkness
And the light could not hold him in bondage.

❄❄❄

Last Foundation

I hear this all the time: "He is gone," "She has gone away."
Yet let me say:
Don't tell me, "He or she is no more."
That is a lie, therefore
It I can't tolerate.
In my soul it penetrates.

Coming and going
To men apart they're standing.
So his language can cope
With only half a hope.
To that ocean I want myself to be uniting
Where is and is-not in their fullness have the same meaning.

❄❄❄❄❄

Śiśu bholānāth, 1922

Rabibār

Som maṅgal budh erā sab
Āse tāḍātāḍi,
Eder ghare āche bujhi
Masta hāoāgāḍi?
Rabibār se kena, mā go,
Eman deri kare?
Dhīre dhīre pouṁchāy se
Sakal bārer pare.
Ākāś pāre tār bāḍiṭi
Dūr ki sabār ceye?
Se bujhi, mā, tomār mato
Garib gharer meye?

Som maṅgal budher kheyāl
Thākbāri janyei,
Bāḍi–pherār dike oder
Ekṭuo man nei.
Rabibārke ke ye eman
Biṣam tāḍā kare,
Ghaṇṭāgulo bājāy yena
Ādh ghaṇṭār pare.
Ākāś–pāre bāḍite tār
Kāj āche sab–ceye.
Se bujhi, mā, tomār mato
Garib–gharer meye.

The Child Bholanath, 1922

Sunday

Monday, Tuesday, Wednesday and all other days
Come fast from far.
In their home, I am sure that each one has
A big motor car!
Mother dear, why does Sunday
Tarry long his ways?
Why does he come so slow,
After the other days,
Unlike others is his home
In the sky away manyfold?
Like you, does his mother come
From a poor household?

When Monday, Tuesday, Wednesday come
As if they mean to stay,
They never think of their homes
And dream of going away.
O mother, why is Sunday always
In such an awful hurry?
The hours seem to strike at half
As if they are in a flurry,
In his home beyond the sky has he
Lot of work on hold?
Like you, does his mother come
From a poor household?

Som maṅgal budher yena
Mukhgulo sab hām̐ḍi,
Choṭo cheler saṅge tāder
Biṣam āḍāāḍi.
Kintu śanir rāter śeṣe
Yemni uṭhi jege,
Rabibārer mukhe dekhi
Hasi āche lege.
Yābār belāy yāy se kem̐de
Moder mukhe ceye.
Se bujhi, mā, tomār mato
Garib–gharer meye.

❄ ❄ ❄

Bāni–binimay

Mā, yadi tui ākāś hatis,
Āmi cām̐pār gāch,
Tor sāthe mor bini–kathāy
Hata kathār nāc.
Tor hāoā mor ḍāle dāle
Kebal theke theke
Kata rakam nācan diye
Āmāy yeta deke.
Mā bale tār sāḍā deba
Kathā kothāy pai,
Pātāy patāy sāḍā āmār
Nece uṭhta tāi.
Tor ālo mor śiśir–phom̐ṭāy
Āmār kāne kāne
Ṭalmaliye ki balta ye

Monday, Tuesday, Wednesday
Have faces glum,
To little kids they never
Become a chum.
But when I awake at the end
Of Saturday night
I see the Sunday greet me
With a smile so bright.
When he says farewell to us
Tears he can't withhold.
Like you, does his mother come
From a poor household?

❄❄❄

Exchange Of Messages

Mother, if you're the sky,
And I, the *champak* tree,
In silence we would go on
A verbal dancing spree.
Your winds through my branches
Passing quite often
Would have danced and called me
Every now and then.
'Mother,' I would want to say
But words would not come
So the dancing of my leaves
My words would become.
On my dewdrops your shining light
Would sway about
And sparkling song would buzz in my
Ears without doubt.

Jhalmalānir gāne.
Āmi takhan phuṭiye ditem
Āmār yata kuṁḍi,
Kathā kaite giye tārā
Nācan dita juḍi.
Uḍo megher chāyāṭi tor
Kothāy theke ese
Āmār chāyāy ghaniye uṭhe
Kothāy yeta bhese.

Sei hata tor bādal belār
Rupkathāṭir mato;
Rajputtur ghar cheḍe yāy
Periye rajya kata;
Sei āmāre bale yeta
Kothāy ālekh–latā,
Sāgarpārer daityapurer
Rājkanyār kathā;
Dekhte petām duorāni̅r
Cakṣu bhara–bhara,
Śiure uṭhe pātā āmār
Kāṁpta tharathara.
Haṭhāt kakhan briṣṭi tomār
Hāoār pāche pāche
Nāmta āmār pātāy pātāy
Ṭāpur–ṭupur nāce;
Sei hata tor kāṁdan–sure
Rāmāyaṇer paḍā,
Sei hata tor gunguniye
Śrāban–diner chaḍā.

Mā, tui hatis ni̅lbarani̅,
Āmi sabuj kāṁca;
Tor hata, mā, ālor hāsi,

I would at once make all my buds
Bloom at their peak
And they would begin to dance
As they try to speak.
Your passing clouds would come,
I would not know from where;
Their shadows would mingle with mine
And then float somewhere.

That would have been like your
Rainy day's fairytale
Where leaving home the prince crosses
Many lands to be on the trail.
He would tell me where
The painted leaves are
And about the princes in the demons'
Den by the ocean far.
I could see the forgotten queen's
Eyes full of tears
And in all my leaves shiver
Would then appear.
All of a sudden the rain would come
On your wind's wing
And fall from leaf to leaf
And start to dance and sing.
That would be your reading the *Ramayana*
In the doleful tune
And the rhymes of the *Sraban* day
That you croon.

Your clothes would be deep blue
Mine a forest green.
Mother, you would have sparkling smile
And my leaves would dance as in spring.

Āmār pātār nācā.
Tor hata, mā, upar theke
Nayan mele cāoā,
Āmār hata āṁkubāṁku
Hāt tule gān gāoā.
Tor hata, mā cirakāler
Tārār manimālā,
Āmār hata dine dine
Phul–phoṭābār pālā.

❄❄❄❄❄

You would look down from above
With eyes wide open,
I would sway and lift my arms
Singing quite often.
You would have the everlasting
Jewelled necklace of stars
Day after day I would have the task of
Blooming my flowers.

❄❄❄❄❄

Pūrabī, 1925

Chabi

Kṣubdha ciṇha eṁke diye śānta sindhubuke
Tarī cale paścimer mukhe.
Ālok–cumbane nīl jal
Kare jhalamal.
Digante megher jāle bijaḍita dinānter moha,
Suryaster śeṣ samāroha.
Ūrdhe yāy dekhā
Tṛtīiār śīrṇa śaśilekhā.
Yena ke ulaṅga śiśu kothāy eseche jāne nā se,
Niḥsaṅkoce hāse.
Bahe manda manthar bātās
Saṅgaśūnya sāyāṇher bairāgya–niḥśvās.
Svargasukhe klānta kon debatār bāśir pūrabī
Śūnyatale dhare ei chabi.
Kṣaṇakāl pare yābe ghuce,
Udāsīn rajanīr kālo keśe sab debe muche.

Emani raṅgr khelā nitya khele ālo ār chāyā,
Emani cañcal māyā
Jīban–ambartale;
Duḥkhe sukhe barṇe barne likhā
Ciṇhahīn padacārī kāler prāntare marīcikā.
Tār pare din yāy, asta yāy rabi;
Yuge yuge muche yāy lakṣa lakṣa rāgrakta chabi.
Tui hethā kabi,
E biśver mṛtyur niḥśās
Āpan bāṁśite bhari gāne tāre bāṁcāite cās.

❄ ❄ ❄

Musical Raga for the Evening, 1925

The Image

Drawing pained lines on the calm ocean's breast
The boat is sailing towards the West.
With the kiss of light the blue waters
Shimmer.
On the horizon the close of the day's spell is caught in the clouds' net,
The last splendour of the sunset.
Above can be seen
The crescent moonbeam
Smiling unabashedly like a naked child who doesn't know
Where she is though.
The languid wind is blowing,
The detached sigh of the lonely evening.
Tired of heaven's bliss, some god's flute plays *purabi's* sadness
And paints this image in the emptiness.
In a short while it will vanish,
All these the indifferent black tresses of the night will banish.

Under life's dome light and shadow everyday
In many colours display,
The fleeting enchantment
Of joy and sorrow's pageant
By a traceless traveller on the sands of time.
Then the days fly, the sunset ending daytime
Through the ages fade endless images drawn with multicoloured palette.
Only you, the poet
Want to keep them alive in the songs of your flute
The world's breath of death's tribute.

❋❋❋

Madhu

Moumāchir mato āmi cāhi nā bhāṇḍār bharibāre
Basantere byartha karibāre.
Se to kabhu pāy nā sandhān
Kothā āche prabhāter paripūrna dān.
Tāhār śrabaṇ bhare
Āpan gunjansvare
Hārāy se nikhiler gān.

Jāne nā phuler gandhe āche kon karun biṣād,
Se jāne tā saṅgraher pather saṅbād.
Cāhe ni se araṇyer pāne,
Latār lābaṇya nāhi jāne,
Paḍe ni phuler barṇe basanter marmabāṇī lekhā.
Madhukaṇā lakṣya tār, tāri kakṣa āche śudhu śekhā.

Pākhir matan man śudhu uḍibār sukh cāhe
Udhāo utsāhe;
Ākāśer bakṣa hate ḍānā bhari tār
Svarṇa–āloker madhu nite cāy, nāhi yār bhār,
Nāhi yār kṣay,
Nāhi yār niruddha sañcay,
Yār bādhā nāi
Yāre pāi tabu nāhi pāi
Yār tare nahe lobh, nahe kṣobh, nahe tikṣṇa riṣ,
Nahe śul, nahe gupta biṣ.

❄❄❄❄❄

Honey

I don't want to fill my store like the bee
So that the spring in vain may be.
He can not discover
Where lies the full gift of morning ever.
His ears are drowned
With his own buzzing sound.
He misses the world's music forever.

He doesn't know what pitiful sorrow is in the flowers' fragrances.
He is all caught up in the gathering of honey he indulges.
The forests he doesn't see,
He doesn't know how graceful vines can be.
In the flowers' colour he doesn't sense spring's message impressed
His aim is fixed on honey and its whereabouts are his only zest.

The mind is like a bird, thirsts for only the pleasure
Of flying through the air.
Its wings want to be filled with honeyed golden light
From the sky's core bright.
That light has no weight, no waning,
No locked up saving,
And which no hindrance can blot.
I get it, yet I do not,
For which there is no greed, no grudge, no envy's abyss,
No sharp pain, no hidden malice.

❄ ❄ ❄ ❄ ❄

Mahuā, 1929

Bicched

Rātri yabe sāṅga hala, dūre calibāre
Dāṁḍāile dvāre.
Āmār kaṇṭher yata gān
Karilām dān.
Tumi hāsi
Mor hāte dile taba biraher bāṁṣi.
Tār pardin hate
Basante śarate
Ākāṣe bātāse uṭhe khed
Keṁde keṁde phire biśve bāṣi ār gāner bicched.

❄❄❄❄❄

Mahua, 1929

Separation

When the night ended you stood at my doorway
Before going far away.
I offered you
All songs my voice knew.
With a smile's tribute
You gave in my hand your separation's flute.
From the next morn
In spring and autumn
Lament fills the air and sky,
Around the world is heard the separation of my song and your flute's cry.

❄❄❄❄❄

Pariśeṣ, 1932

Praśna

Bhagabān, tumi yuge yuge dūt, pāṭhāyecha bāre bāre
Dayāhīn saṁsāre,
Tārā bale gela 'ksamā karo sabe', bale gela 'bhālobāso—
Antar hate bidveṣbiṣ nāśo'.
Baraniya tārā, smaraṇiya tārā, tabuo bāhir–dvāre
Āji durdine phirānu tāder byartha namaskāre.

Āmi–ye dekhechi gopan hiṁsā kapaṭ rātrichāye
Heneche niḥsahāye,
Āmi–ye dekhechi pratikārhīn śakter aparādhe
Bicārer bāṇī nirabe nibhṛte kāṁde.
Āmi–ye dekhinu taruṇ bālak unmād haye chuṭe
Ki yantranāy mareche pāthare nisphal māthā kuṭe.

Kaṇṭha āmār ruddha ājike, bāṁṣi saṅgit hārā,
Amābasyār kārā
Lupta kareche āmār bhuban duḥsvapaner tale,
Tāi to tomāy śudhāi aśrujale—
Jāhārā tomār biṣāiche bāyu, nibhāiche taba ālo,
Tumi ki tāder kṣamā kariācha, tumi ki besecha bhālo.

❄❄❄❄❄

The End, 1932

The Question

Time and again You have sent to this pitiless world,
My lord, Your many prophets, saints and sages.
"Love all, forgive, and rid your hearts of the venom
Of violence," they told through the ages.
Worthy of remembrance and adoration
Though they are, yet in these times so hard
With my vain tribute and salutation
I turn them away from my courtyard.

For I've seen covert violence
In the cloak of night's darkness
Slaughtering the weak and the helpless.
I have seen justice crying in the wilderness
    For the inequity of the mighty.
I have seen helpless children beating their
    Heads against hearts of stone without pity.

Today my voice is choked,
    My flute is mute. Despair—
An abyss of darkness drowns
    My world in untold nightmare.
"Have You forgiven and loved,"
    I ask my Lord, as I shed a tear,
"Those who snuffed Your light
    And poisoned Your atmosphere?"

❄ ❄ ❄ ❄ ❄

Pūnaśca, 1932

Patralekhā

Dile tumi sonā–moḍā phounṭain pen,
Kata mato lekhār asbāb.
Choṭo desk khāni
Ākhroṭ kaṭh diye gaḍā.
Chāp mārā ciṭhir kāgaj
Nānā bāhārer.
Rūpor kāgaj–kāṭā, enāmel–karā.
Kāṁci churi gālā lāl–phite.
Kāṁcer kāgaj–cāpā,
Lāl nīl sabuj pencil.
Bale giyechile tumi ciṭhi lekhā cāi
Ekdin pare pare.

Likhte basechi ciṭhi,
Sakālei snān haye geche.

Likhi ye ki katha niye kichutei bhebe pāi ne to.
Ekṭi khabar āche śudhu—
Tumi cale gecha.
Se khabar tomār to jānā.
Tabu mane hay,
Bhālo kare tumi se jāno nā.
Tāi bhābi e kathāṭi jānāi tomāke —
Tumi cale gecha.
Yatabār lekhā ṣuru kari
Tatabār dharā paḍe e khabar sahaj to nay.
Āmi nai kabi,
Bhāṣār bhitare āmi kanṭhasvar pāri ne to dite;
Nā thāke cokher cāoā.
Yata likhi tata chiṁḍe pheli.

Postscript, 1932

Writing A Letter

You gave me a gold-capped fountain pen
And so many other things for my writing.
A small desk
Made of walnut,
A letter pad, printed with
Many designs,
A silver letter-opener, enamelled;
Scissors, pen-knife, lacquer, red tape,
A glass paper-weight and
Red, blue, green pencils.
You told I must write you a letter
Every other day.

I am sitting down to write a letter.
By the way I took my bath in the morning.

I can't decide what I shall write about.
There is only one news item–
You have left.
But you already know it.
Yet I think
You don't know it very well.
That's why I think of telling you that—
You have left.
No matter how many times I begin
Each time I find that the news isn't so simple to write.
A poet I am not,
I can't infuse the words with my voice;
Nor add my look to them.
So each time I write I tear it up.

Daśṭā to beje gala.
Tomār bhāipo baku yābe iskule,
Yāi tāke khāiye āsige.
Śeṣbār ei likhe yāi —
Tumi cale gecha.
Bāki ār yata kichu
Hijibiji āṁkājokā blaṭiṅer pare.

❄ ❄ ❄

Aparādhī

Tumi bala Tinu praśray pāy āmār kāche —
Tāi rāg karo tumi.
Oke bhālobāsi,
Tāi oke duṣṭu bale dekhi,
Doṣī bale dekhi ne —
Rāgo kari or pare
Bhālao lāge oke,
E katahāṭā miche nay hayto.
Ek–ekjan mānuṣ aman thāke
Se lok nehāt manda nay,
Seijanyei sahaje tār mandaṭāi paḍe dharā.
Se hatabhāgā raṅe manda, kintu manda nay rase;
Tār doṣ stupe beśi,
Bhāre beśi nay;
Tāi dekhte yataṭā lāge,
Gāye lage nā tata.
Manṭā or hālkā chipchipe nouko,
Huhu kare cale yāy bhese;
E pārer bojhā o pāre cālān kare dey
Dekhte dekhte;
Oke kichui cāp daya nā,
Temni o deya nā cāp.

O, it is past ten now.
Your nephew, Baku, must go to school.
Let me go and serve his food.
For the last time I write this –
You have left.
All the rest are
Scribbles, doodle marks on a blotting paper.

❄ ❄ ❄

The Guilty

You say I pamper Teenu –
that upsets you.
I love him,
that's why I think he is naughty,
I don't consider him to be guilty.
Sometimes I too get upset with him,
then again I also like him,
this is perhaps not the untruth.
Some people are like that.
The person may not be all bad,
that's why the bad in him catches the eye easily.
The poor soul may be bad in appearance but not in humour;
his faults may have volume
but not weight;
they may appear to be heavy
but not so when shouldered.
His mind is light, and like a slim boat
floats away very fast;
like it or not
doesn't stay in the same place for long,
transfers baggage from one bank to the other in a flash.
Nothing presses upon him;
he doesn't press upon anyone either.

Svābhāb or āsar jamāno,
Kathā kay bistar,
Tāi bistar miche balte hay—
Naile phāṁk pare kathār ṭhās–bunonite.
Micheṭā nay or mane,
Se or bhāṣāy.
Or byākaraṇṭā yār jānā
Tār bujhte hay nā deri.
Oke tumi bala ninduk,— tā satya.
Satyake bāḍiye tule bāṁkiye diye o ninde bānāy—
Yār ninde kare tār manda habe bale nay,
Yārā ninde śone tāder bhālo lāgbe bale.
Tārā āche samasta saṁsār juḍe.
Tārā ninder nihārikā,
O hala ninder tārā,
Or jyoti tāderi kāch theke paoā.
Āsal kathā or buddhi āche, nei bebecanā.
Tāi or aparādh niye hāsi cale.
Yārā bhalomanda bibecanā kare sukṣma touler māpe
Tāder dekhe hāsi yāy bandha haye;
Tader saṅgaṭā ojane hay bhārī,
Say nā beśikṣan;
Daibe tāder truṭi yadi hay asābdhāne
Hāṁp cheḍe bāṁce loke.

Bujhiye bali kāke bale abibecanā.—
Mākhan laksmichāḍāṭā sanskriter claśe
Coukite lāgiye rekhechila bhuso;
Chāp legechila panditmaśāyer jāmār piṭhe;
Se hesechila, sabāi hesechila
Panditmaśāy chāḍā.
Headmaster dilen cheleṭāke ekebāre taḍiye;
Tini atyanta gambhir, tini atyanta bibecak.
Taṁr bhāb–gatik dekhe hāsi bandha haye yāy.

His nature is to brighten up a party.
He talks too much,
that's why he lies much –
otherwise the story won't be neatly woven, and have flaws.
But these lies don't come from his mind;
they are in his language.
He who knows his nature
doesn't take long to recognise it.
You say that he speaks ill of others, — that's true.
By twisting and embellishing the truth he speaks ill.
His intent is not to harm the person he is speaking ill of,
rather to please those who like listening to slanders.
These people are all over the world.
They are the nebulae of slanders;
he is only a star of slanders.
He gets his glow from them.
The truth is that he has got intelligence, not judgement.
That's why people laugh at his speaking ill of others.
Those who very carefully weigh good and bad—
laughter stops at their gaze.
Their company hangs heavy,
can't be tolerated for long.
If by chance such people are remiss in catching something
others sigh a sigh of relief.

Let me explain what is meant by lack of judgement.
In our Sanskrit class the mischievous Makhan
smeared soot on the chair's back.
It left an imprint on the back of the teacher's shirt.
Makhan laughed. Everyone laughed,
except the teacher.
The headmaster expelled the boy;
he was serious and severe in his judgement.
His demeanour stops all laughter.

Tinu apakār kare kichu nā bhebe,
Upakār kare anāyāse
Konotāi mane rākhe nā.
O dhār neya, kheāl nei śodh karbār;
Yārā dhār neya or cāche
Pāonār talab nei tāder darjāy.
Moṭer upar ori loksān hay beśī.

Tomāke āmi bali, oke gāl dio yā khuśī,
Ābār heso mane mane—
Naile bhul habe.
Āmi oke dekhi kācher theke, mānuṣ bale,
Bhālomanda periye.
Tumi dekha dūre base, biśeṣaṇer kaṭhgaḍāy oke khāḍā rekhe.
Āmi oke lāṇchana dei tomār ceye beṣi,—
Kṣamā kari tomār ceye baḍo kare.
Sājā dei, nirbāsan dei ne.
O āmār kāchei raye gela,
Rāg koro nā tai niye.

* * *

Dekhā

Moṭā moṭā kālo megh
Klānta pāloāner dal yena,
Samasta rāt barsaner par
Ākāśer ek pāśe ese jamla
Ghemsāghemsi kare.
Bāgāner dakṣiṇ sīmāy segun gāche
Mañjarir ḍheugulote haṭhāt paḍla ālo,
Camke uṭhla baner cāyā.

Teenu doesn't harm anyone with motive;
helping others comes easy for him,
And he doesn't keep either in his mind.
He borrows, doesn't remember to pay back,
but those who borrow from him
don't see him at their doorstep demanding payment either.
On the whole his loss is greater.

Let me say, rebuke him as much as you want
and then laugh within yourself –
otherwise it would be wrong.
I see him close, as a human,
ignoring his good and bad.
You see him from a distance, scrutinising his qualities.
I chastise him more than you do,
I also forgive him much more.
I punish him, but don't exile him.
Let him stay with me
and don't be offended by it.

❄ ❄ ❄

Observation

After pouring through the night
Dark heavy clouds,
Like a band of tired wrestlers,
Were bunched together
In one end of the sky.
Startling the forest's shadows.
suddenly light fell upon the blossoms
of the teakwood trees
at the south-end of the garden.

Śrāban̤ māser roudra dekhā diyeche
Ānāhūta atithi,
Hāsir kolāhal uṭhla
Gāche gache ḍāle–pālāy.
Rod–pohāno bhābnāgulo
Bhese bhese beḍālo maner dūr gagane.
Belā gela akāje.

Bikele haṭhat ela guruguru dhvani,
Kār yena sanket.
Ek muhūrte megher dal
Buk phuliye hu hu kare chuṭe āse
Tāder koṇ cheḍe.
Bām̐dher jal haye gela kālo,
Baṭer talāy nāmla thamthame andhakār.
Dur baner pātāy pātāy
Beje oṭhe dhārā pataner bhūmikā.

Dekhte dekhte ghanabriṣṭite pāndur haye āse
Samasta ākāś,
Māṭh bhese yāy jale.
Buḍo buḍo gāchgulo āluthālu mātāmāti kare
Chelemānuṣer mato;
Dhairya thāke nā tāler pātāy, bām̐śer ḍāle.
Ekṭu parei pālā hala śeṣ,
Ākāś nikiye gela ke.
Kriṣñapakṣer kriśa cānd yena rogaśajyā cheḍe
Klānta hāsi niye angane bāhir haye ela.

Man bale, ei āmār yata dekhār ṭukro
Cāi ne hārāte.
Āmār sattar bacharer kheyāy
Kata calti muhūrta uṭhe basechila
Tārā pār haye geche adṛśye.
Tār madhye duṭi ekṭi kuḍemir dinke

The sunshine of the *Sraban* month appeared
as an uninvited guest,
waves of laughter rolled
from tree to tree, branch to branch.
My thoughts, basking in that sunshine,
floated in the far end of my mind's sky.
The day was whiled away.

In the afternoon suddenly came the rumbling sound
As if it was a sign from someone.
In a moment the horde of clouds,
puffing their chests,
came running from their corner.
The water of the dam turned black,
glum darkness descended under the *peepul*-tree.
The prologue of rainfall sounded
at a distance in the leaves in the forest.

In no time at all, the heavy rain darkened
the whole sky,
and water flooded the meadow.
The full-grown trees engaged in romping naughtiness
like little children;
the palm leaves, the bamboo branches lost their patience.
In a little while the drama ended.
Someone wiped the sky clean.
The thin moon of the dark fortnight, as if from a sickbed,
appeared in the yard wearing a pale smile.

My mind says all these little observations
I don't want to lose.
Many fleeting moments were in my seventy-year ferryboat
and then they vanished.
From them I'll leave behind
one or two lazy days,

Pichane rekhe yāba
Chande gāṁthā kuḍemir kārukāje,
Tārā jāniye debe āśćarya kathāṭi,—
Ekdin āmi dekhechilem ei sab–kichu.

❄❄❄

Sundar

Plātināmer aṅṭir mājhkhāne yena hīre.
Ākāśer sīmā ghire megh,
Mājhkhāner roddur āsche māṭher upar.
Hu hu kare baiche hāoā,
Peṁpe gāchgulor yena ātanka legeche,
Uttarer māṭhe nimgāche bedheche bidroha,
Tālgāchgulor māthāy bistar bakuni.
Belā ekhan āḍāiṭā.
Bhije baner jhalmale madhānya
Uttar dakṣiner jānālā diye ese
Juḍe baseche āmār samasta man.

Jani ne kena mane hay,
Ei din dur kāler ār kono–ekṭā diner mato.
E rakam din māne nā kono dāyke,
Er kāche kichui nei jaruri,
Bartamāner noṅar–cheṁḍā bhese–yāoā ei din.
Eke dekhechi atīter marīcikā bale
Se atīt ki chila kono kāle konokhāne,
Se ki cira yugeri atīt nay.
Preyasīke mane hay se āmār janmajanmāntarer janā—
Ye kāle svarga, ye kāle satyayug,
Ye kāl sakal yugeri dharā–choṁār bāire.

woven as a tapestry with the rhymes of my idleness.
They would declare the message, —
there were days when I observed all these.

❄ ❄ ❄

Beautiful

Just like a diamond ring in platinum setting,
Clouds are all around the sky's edge and
through an opening in the middle sunshine falls on the meadow.
Strong wind is blowing,
distress seem to have struck the papaya trees,
some uprising is taking place in the *neem*-tree in north-end
and thrashings abound on the palm tree-heads.
It is two-thirty in the afternoon now.
The shinning midday from the rain-soaked forest
has come through the north and south windows
and spread its seat on my entire mind.

I don't know why it happens so,
this day seems like one other day from a time long past.
Such a day is bound by no obligation,
nothing is pressing to it,
unanchored in the present and afloat.
The past, as whose mirage this day appeared to be
was it in some other place in some other bygone days,
or is it not the past of all ages?
My beloved seems to be known to me for many aeons, —
from the time of paradise, the first cycle of time,
a time beyond the touch and grasp of all times.

Temni ei ye sonāy pannāy chayāy aloy gāṁthā
Ākaśer neśāy manthar āṣdḥer din
Bihval haye āche māṭher opar oḍnā chaḍiye diye,
Er mādhurīkeo mane hay āche tabu nei,
Ei ākāśbīnāy gouḍsāraṅer ālāp,
Se ālāp āche sarbakāler nepathya theke.

❄ ❄ ❄

Kyāmeliā

Nām tār kamalā,
Dekhechi tār khātār upare lekhā.
Se calechila trāme, tār bhāike niye kalejer rāstāy.
Āmi chilām pichaner beñcite.
Mukher ek pāśer niṭol rekhāṭi dekhā yāy,
Ār ghāḍer upar komal culguli khoṁpār nice.
Kole tār chila bai ār khātā.
Yekhāne āmār nambār sekhāne nāmā hala nā.
Ekhan theke samayer hisāb kare beroi—
Se hisāb āmār kājer saṅge ṭhikṭi mele nā,
Prāy ṭhik mele oder berobār samayer saṅge,
Prāyei hay dekhā.
Mane mane bhābi, ār–kono sambandha nā thāk
O to āmār sahayātriṇī.
Nirmal buddhir cehārā
Jhakjhak karche yena.
Sukumār kapāl theke cul upare tolā,
Ujjval cokher driṣṭi niḥsaṁkoc.
Mane bhābi ekṭā–kono saṅkaṭ dekhā dey nā kena,
Uddhār kare janma sarthak kari—
Rāstār madhye ekṭā kono utpāt,
Kono–ekjan guṇḍār spardhā.
Eman to ājkāl ghaṭei thāke.

Its charm, its beauty seems to be here and yet it is not.
So is this day of *Ashadh*, woven with gold and emerald,
light and shadow, slow-paced with leisure,
is beside itself after spreading its scarf on the meadow.
It is like the slow movement of the melody *gaudsarang* in heaven's harp.
This slow movement of the melody comes from behind the curtain of all times.

❄❄❄

Camellia

Her name is Kamala,
I've seen it written on her notebook.
She was on the streetcar, going to college with her brother.
I was in the row behind.
I could see the perfect outline of one side of her face,
and the soft hairs on her neck under the bun.
On her lap were her books and notebook.
I couldn't get off at my stop.
Since then I computed my time before getting out—
which didn't quite fit with my work schedule
but matched the time of their going.
I saw her quite often.
I thought, even though there was no connection,
at least she was my co-passenger.
Her appearance showed pure intellect
as if it was radiating.
Her hair combed away from her tender forehead,
unabashed and bright was the look on her eyes.
I imagined some sort of crisis happening,
then blessed would be my birth by rescuing her—
say, some kind of disturbance,
or a ruffian's outrage.
Such happenings are quite common these days.

Kintu āmār bhāgyaṭā yena gholā jaler dobā,
Baḍo rakam itihās dhare nā tār madhye,
Nirīha dingulo byaṅer mato ekgheye ḍāke,
Nā sekhāne haṅar–kunirer nimantraṇ, nā rājhāṁser.

Ekdin chila ṭhelāṭheli bhiḍ,
Kamalār pāśe baseche ekjan ādhā–iṁrej.
Icche karchila, akāraṇe ṭupiṭā uḍiye deyi tār māthā theke,
Ghāḍe dhare tāke rāstāy dei nāmiye.
Kono chuto pāi ne, hāt niśpiś kare.
Eman samay se ekṭā moṭā curoṭ dhariye
Ṭānte karle śuru.
Kāche ese ballum, 'Phelo curoṭ.'
Yena peleyi nā śunte,
Dhoṁā oḍāte lagla beś ghorālo kare.
Mukh theke ṭene phele dilem curoṭ rāstāy.
Hāte muṭho pākiye ekbār takālo kaṭmaṭ kare—
Ār kichu balle nā, ek lāphe neme gela.
Bodh hay āmāke cene.
Āmār nām āche phuṭbal khelāy,
Beś ekṭu caoḍā gocher nām.
Lāl haye uṭhla meyeṭir mukh,
Bai khule māthā nicu kare bhān karle paḍbār.
Hat kāṁpte lāgla,
Kaṭākṣeo tākāle nā bīrpuruṣer dike.
Āpiser baburā balle, 'beś karechen maśāy.'
Ekṭu parei meyeṭi neme paḍla ajāygāy,
Ektā tyāksi kare gela cale.

Pardin tāke dekhlum nā,
Tār pardino nā,
Tṛtiya dine dekhi
Ekṭā thelāgaḍite caleche kaleje.
Bujhlum, bhul karechi goṁārer mato.
O meye nijer dāy nijei pāre nite,
Āmāke kono darkāri chila nā.

But my fate was like a muddy puddle,
there was no room for an epoch making story;
the uneventful days monotonously croaked like frogs.
Sharks, crocodiles were uninvited there, as were the swans.

One day the streetcar was packed with crowds.
An Anglo-Indian was sitting next to Kamala.
I had an urge to knock off the hat from his head, unprovoked,
grab him by the collar and throw him out on the road.
I found no excuse and my hands were itching.
Just at that moment he lit a fat cigar
and started smoking.
Coming near him I said, "Throw away the cigar."
He continued billowing smoke, as if he hadn't heard me.
I snatched the cigar from his mouth
and threw it on the road.
Just once he made a fist and gave me an angry look—
but said nothing. He got down from the car in a leap.
Perhaps he recognised me.
I was a household name in soccer,
A big one, in fact.
The girl's face turned red.
She opened her book and with eyes lowered pretended to
read.
Her hands were trembling.
She didn't give even a side-glance at her hero.
The office-going crowd said, "You've done the right thing."
A little while later the girl got off at a different stop,
and left in a taxi.

Next day I didn't see her,
Nor the day after.
On the third day I saw her going to college in a rickshaw.
I understood what a blunder I had done in rage.
This girl was quite capable of taking care of herself,

Ābār ballum mane mane,
Bhāgyaṭā gholā jaler ḍobā—
B̄iratver smṛti maner madhye kebali āj aoāj karche
Kolābyāṅer ṭhaṭṭār mato.
Ṭhik karlum, bhul śodhrāte habe.

Khabar peyechi garamer chuṭite orā yāy dārjiliṅe.
Sebār āmāro hāoā badlābār jaruri darkār.
Oder choṭṭa bāsā, nām diyeche matiyā—
Rāstā theke ekṭu neme ek koṇe
Gācher āḍāle,
Sāmne barapher pāhāḍ.
Śonā gela āsbe nā ebār.
Phirba mane karchi eman samaye āmār ek bhakter saṅge dekhā, Mohanlāl—
Rogā mānuṣṭi, lambā, cokhe caśmā,
Durbal pākyantra darjiliṅer hāoāy ekṭu utsāha pāy.
Se balle, "tanukā āmār bon,
Kichute chaḍbe nā tomār saṅge dekhā nā kare."
Meyeṭi chāyār mato,
Deha yataṭuku nā hale nay tataṭuku—
Yataṭā paḍāsonāy jhoṁk, āhāre tataṭā nay.
Phuṭbaler sardārer pare tāi eta adbhut bhakti—
Mane karle, ālāp karte esechi se āmār durlav dayā.
Hāy re bhāgyer khelā.

Yedin neme āsba tār du din āge tanukā balle,
'Ekṭi jiniṣ deba āpnāke, yāte mane thākbe āmāder kathā—
Ekṭi phuler gāch.'
E ek utpāt. Cup kare railem.
Tanukā balle, 'dāmi durlav gāch,
E deśer māṭite anek yatne bāṁce.'
Jiges karlem, 'nāmṭā kī?'
Se balle, 'kyāmeliā.'

She didn't need me.
Again I thought in my mind
how my fate was like a muddy puddle—
where the memory of my bravery quite often croaked
like the bull frog joke.
I decided to make amends.

I gathered that they went to Darjeeling during summer vacation.
That year a change of climate became urgent for me as well.
Their house was small; they named it *Motiya.*
It was down the road in a corner,
shaded by trees,
and facing snowy mountain peaks.
Arriving there, I heard they wouldn't come that year.
I was thinking of returning when I met an admirer of mine,
Mohanlal.
Sickly man he was, tall, with eye glasses,
his weak digestion needed Darjeeling's stimulation.
He said, "My sister, Tanuka,
Won't let you go without meeting her."
Shadow of a girl she was,
minimal was her body,
her interest in food wasn't as much as that in her studies.
That explained her strange interest in a leading soccer player.
She took my visiting her as some rare kindness on my part.
Alas, what an irony of fate it was!

Two days before my departure Tanuka said,
"I would present you something to remember us—
a flowering plant."
I thought of it as a burden but kept silent.
Tanuka said, "It's a precious and rare plant.
It survives in our land with extreme care."
I asked, "What's its name?'

Camak lāgla—
Ār ekṭā nām jhalak diye uṭhla maner andhakāre.
Hese ballem, 'kyāmeliā,
Sahaje bujhi er man mele nā.'
Tanukā ki bujhle jānine, haṭhat lajjā pele,
Khuśio hala.
Callem tabsudda gāch niye.
Dekhā gela, pārśabartinī hisābe sahayātriṇīṭi sahaj nay.
Ekṭā do–kāmra gaḍite
Tabṭāke lukolem nābār ghare.
Thāk ei bhramaṇ bṛtanta,
Bād deoā jāk āro mās kayeker tucchatā.

Pujor chuṭite prahasaner yabanikā uṭhla
Sāṁotāl parganāy.
Jāygāṭā choṭo. Nām balte cāi ne—
Bāyubadaler bāyu–grastadal e jāygār khabar jāne nā.
Kamalār māmā chilen reler enginiār.
Eikhāne bāsā beṁdhechen
Śālbaner chāyāy, kaṭhbiḍālider pāḍāy.
Sekhāne nīl pāhāḍ dekhā yāy digante,
Adūre jaladhārā caleche bālir madhya diye,
Palāṣbane tasarer guṭi dhareche,
Mahiṣ carche hartaki gācher talāy—
Ulaṅga sāṁotāler chele piṭher upare.
Bāsābāḍi kothāo nei,
Tāi tābu pātlem nadir dhāre.
Saṅgi chila nā keu,
Kebal chila tabe sei kyāmeliā.

Kamalā eseche māke niye.
Rod oṭhbār āge
Hime–choṁāy snigdha hāoāy
Śāl–bāgāner bhitar diye beḍāte yāy chāti hāte.
Meṭho phulgulo pāye ese māthā koṭe,
Kintu se ki ceye dekhe.

She said, "Camellia."
It startled me,
Another name flashed in the darkness of my mind.
I said with a smile, "Camellia,
It isn't easy to win her heart, I suppose."
I didn't know what Tanuka thought. She was abashed
and happy too.
I started my journey with the potted plant
and found that my travel mate was not an easy neighbour.
In the two-room compartment
I placed the pot in the bathroom.
Forget my travel story,
Skip a few more moths of triviality too.

The curtain of this farce rose during the *Puja* holidays
in the Santhal Parganas.
It is a small place. I don't want to tell its name.
It is still unknown to the change-of-air fanatics.
Kamala's maternal uncle, a railway engineer,
had his quarters there
in the shade of *shal* forest, where the squirrels nest.
The blue-hill-range could be seen in the horizon,
a stream ran through the sand not far away.
Silkworms' cocoons were forming in the *palash* forests.
Buffaloes, carrying the naked *santhal* children
on their back grazed under the myrobalan trees
No settlement was in sight,
so I pitched my tent near the riverbank.
I had no other companion
but the potted camellia.

Kamala was visiting with her mother.
In the dewy cool air,
before the sun got hot,
with a parasol in hand, she went for walk through the *shal* forest.
The ground-cover flowers paid homage to her feet,

Alpa jal nadi pāye hemṭe
Periye yāy o pāre,
Sekhāne śiśugācher talāy bai paḍe.
Ār āmāke ye cineche
Tā janlām āmāke lakṣya kare nā balei.

Ekdin dekhi, nadīr dhāre bālir upar caḍibhāti karche erā.
Icche hala giye bali, āmāke darkār ki nei kichutei.
Āmi pāri jal tule ānte nadi theke—
Pāri ban theke kaṭh ante keṭe,
Ār, tā chāḍā kāchākāchi jaṅgaler madhye
Ekṭā bhadragocher bhāluko ki mele nā.

Dekhlem daler madhye ekjan yubak—
Śorṭ–parā, gāye reśamer biliti jāmā,
Kamalār paśe pā chaḍiye
Hābhānā curoṭ khācche.
Ār kamalā anyamane ṭukro ṭukro karche
Ekṭā śvetjabār papḍi,
Pāśe paḍe āche
Biliti masik patra.

Muhurte bujhlem ei sāṁotāl parganār nirjan kone
Āmi asahya atirikta, dharbe nā kothāo.
Takhani cale yetem, kintu bāki āche ekṭi kāj.
Ār din–kayekei kyāmeliā phuṭbe,
Pāṭhiye diye tabe chuṭi.
Samasta din banduk ghāḍe śikāre phiri bane jaṅgale,
Sandhyār āge phire ese ṭabe dei jal
Ār dekhi kuḍi egola kata dūr.

Samay hayeche āj.
Ye āne āmār rānnār kaṭh
Ḍekechi sei sāotāl meyeṭike.
Tār hāt diye pāṭhāba
Śālpātār patre.

but did she even glance at them?
She crossed the shallow stream on her feet
to the other shore,
where she read a book under a *shishu* tree.
The fact that she had recognised me
was clear from her not even glancing at me.

One day I found them picnicking on the sandy riverbank.
I wished to go there and ask if they needed my help at all.
I could fetch water from the river,
hew firewood from the forest.
Or in the nearby jungle couldn't there be
at least one well behaved bear?

I noticed a young man in their party,
in shorts and wearing a silk shirt of foreign make.
With his legs outstretched he was sitting beside Kamala
and smoking a Havana cigar.
Kamala was absent-mindedly shredding
the petals of a white hibiscus.
Beside her lay
An English monthly magazine.

Instantly I realised that in that solitary corner of the *Santhal Parganas*
I was intolerable, superfluous and there was no room for me.
I would have left at once, but one task was still undone.
In a few days the camellia would flower.
I'd leave after sending it to her.
All day long I went hunting in the forest with my gun,
returning before sunset to water the potted plant
and to see how far the bud had come along.

The day was at hand.
I sent for the *Santhal* girl
who fetches fire logs for my cooking.
I would send it through her

Tāṁbur madhye base takhan paḍchi ḍiṭektibh galpa.
Bāire theke miṣṭisure āoāj ela, 'bābu, dekechis kene.'
Beriye ese dekhi kyāmeliā
Sāṁotāl meyer kāne,
Kālo gāler upar ālo kareche.
Se ābār jiges karle, 'dekechis kene.'
Āmi ballem, 'ei janyei.'
Tār pare phire elem kalkātāy.

❄ ❄ ❄

Bāṁśi

Kinu goālār gali.
Dotalā bāḍir
Lohār–garāde–deoā ektalā ghar
Pather dhārei.
Lonā–dharā deoālete mājhe mājhe dhase geche bāli,
Mājhe mājhe syṁātā–paḍā dāg.
Mārkin thāner mārkā ekkhānā chabi
Siddhidātā gaṇeśer
Darjār pare āṁṭā.
Āmi chāḍā ghare thāke ārekṭā jib
Ek bhāḍātei,
Seṭā ṭikṭiki.
Taphāt āmār saṅge ei śudhu
Nei tār anner abhāb.

Betan paṁciś ṭākā,
Sadagari apiser kaniṣṭha kerāni.
Khete pāi dattader bāḍi
Cheleke paḍiye.
Śeyāldā isṭiśane yāi,
Sandheṭā kāṭiye āsi,
Ālo jvālbār day bāṁce.

on a plate made from *shal* leaves.
I was reading a detective story in my tent.
A sweet voice called from outside, "Why have you called me, sir?"
I came out and saw that the camellia
was adorning the Santhal girl's ear,
lighting up her dark cheek.
Again she asked, "Why did you call?"
I said, "Just for that."
Then I returned to Calcutta.

❄ ❄ ❄

The Flute

I live in the Kinu milkman's alley.
My room, with its iron railings,
is near the road
and in a two-story house.
The wall is decrepit, even the cement is crumbling due to salt,
dark marks of dampness here and there.
A cheap poster-like drawing
of *Ganesha*, the lord of success, the likeness stamped
on a raw cotton cloth, adorns the door.
Along with me there is another creature
in my room. His rent is included in mine:
he is a lizard.
The difference between him and me is this:
he has no want of food.

As a junior clerk in a merchant's office
my salary is twenty-five rupees a month.
My food is provided by the Dutta household
for tutoring their son.
I spend my evenings
in the *Sealdah* station

Enjiner dhas dhas,
Bāṁśir āoāj,
Yatrir byastatā,
Kuli–hāṁkahāṁki.
sāḍe daś beje yāy,
Tār pare ghare ese nirālā niḥjhum andhakār.

Dhaleśvarinaditire pisider grām.
Tār deorer meye,
Abhāgār sāthe tār bibāher chila ṭhikṭhak.
Lagna śubha, niścita pramān pāoā gela—
Sei lagne esechi pāliye.
Meyeṭā to rakṣā pele,
Āmi tathaibaca.
Gharete ela nā se to, mane tār nitya āsājāoā—
Paḍane dhākāi śāḍi, kapāle siṁdur.

Barṣā ghana ghor.
Trāmer kharcā bāḍe,
Mājhe mājhe māineo kāṭā yāy
Galiṭār koṇe koṇe
Jame oṭhe pace oṭhe
Āmer khosā o āṁṭi, kāṁṭhāler bhuti,
Mācher kānkā,
Marā biḍāler chānā,
Chāipāṁś āro kata ki ye
Chātār absthākhānā jarimānā–deoā
Māiner mato,
Bahu chidra tār.
Apiser saj
Gopikānta gosāṁiyer manṭā yeman,
Sarbadāi rasasikta thāke.

to save the cost of light.
The noise of engines chuffing,
whistles blowing,
passengers bustling,
hubbub of porters –
time passes in unending clamour.
Then after ten-thirty
I come to the loneliness, absolute silence
and darkness of my room.

My aunt's village is on the bank of the *Dhaleswari* river.
Her brother-in-law's daughter's marriage
was arranged with this luckless one.
The unmistakable signs of the auspicious hour were there.
I ran away at that very moment.
The girl was saved,
so was I.
She didn't come to my home, but she comes to my mind all the time—
wearing a *Dhakai-sari* and a vermilion dot adorning her forehead.

It is the season of heavy rain.
The cost of riding streetcar mounts;
every now and then my pay is also docked.
In the nooks and crannies of the alley —
mango peels and stones, discards of jack-fruit,
gills of fish,
a dead kitten maybe and
much more trash gather and rot.
The condition of my umbrella is like a salary
that has been docked too many times —
full of holes.
My office-attire

Bādaler kālo chāyā
Syāṁtsyāṁte ghar̤tāte dhuke
Kale–paḍā jantur matan
Murchāy asāḍ.
Din–rāt mane hay, kon ādhmarā
Jagater saṅge yena āṣṭepṛṣthe bāṁdhā paḍe āchi.

Galir moḍei thāke kāntabābu,
Yatne–pāṭ–karā lambā cul,
Baḍo baḍo cokh,
Śoukhin mejāj.
Karneṭ bājāno tār sakh.
Mājhe mājhe sur jege oṭhe
E galir bibhatsa bātāse—
Kakhano gabhīr rāte,
Bhorbelā ādho andhakāre,
Kakhano baikāle
Jhikimiki āloy chāyay.
Haṭhāt sandhyāy
Sindhu–baṁroyāy lāge tān,
Samasta ākaśe bāje
Anādi kāler biraha bedanā.
Takhani muhūrte dharā paḍe
E galiṭā ghor miche,
Durbisaha, mātāler pralāper mato.
Haṭhāt khabar pāi mane
Ākbar bādśār saṅge
Haripada kerānir kono bhed nei.
Bāṁśir karun dāk beye
Cheṁḍā chātā rājchatra mile cale geche
Ek baikuṇṭher dike.

is like the *Krishna* devotee, Gopikanta Gosain,
ever pining in anguish.
The dark shadow of rain-clouds
in my damp room
is in a lifeless swoon
like an animal caught in a snare.
All day and night it seems to me that I'm
fastened fast to some half-dead world.

Kantababu lives where the lane takes a turn,
carefully groomed is his long hair,
big eyes,
and refined taste.
Playing clarinet is his hobby.
Every now and then its melody fills
the foul air of the alley —-
sometimes in the dead of night,
in the semi-darkness of the dawn,
sometimes in the afternoon's
shimmering light and shadow.
Suddenly at the dusk the tune of *Sindhu-baroa*
fills the sky
with the eternal pain of lovers-apart.
Instantly it seems
this alley is utterly unreal
and as intolerable as the delirium of a drunk.
Suddenly a report comes to my mind
that there is not the slightest difference
between the Emperor Akbar and this Haripada clerk.
With the doleful tune of the flute
my tattered umbrella becomes a king's sunshade
floating towards some paradise.

E gān yekhāne satya
Ananta godhūlilagne
Seikhāne
Bahi cale dhaleśvari,
T̄ire tamāler ghana chāyā;
Āṅināte
Ye āche apekṣā kare, tār
Parane ḍhākāi śāḍi, kapāle siṁdur.

❄ ❄ ❄ ❄ ❄

This tune is real
where in an endless
twilight hour
flows the *Dhaleswari.*
On her bank is the deep shadow of the palm trees,
in the courtyard awaits for me the one
wearing a *Dhakai-sari* and a vermilion dot on her forehead.

❄ ❄ ❄ ❄ ❄

Bicitritā, 1932

Acenā

Tomāre āmi kakhano cini nāko,
Lukāno naha, tabu lukāno thāka.
    Chabir mato bhābanā paraśiā
    Ekṭu ācha manere haraṣiā.

Anek din diyecha tumi dekhā,
Basecha pāśe, tabuo āmi ekā.
    Āmār kāche rahile bideśinī,
    Laile śudhu nayan mama jini.

Bedanā kichu āche taba mane,
Se byathā dhāke tomāre ābaraṇe.
    Śunya–pāne cāhiyā thāka tumi,
    Niśvāsiyā uṭhe kānanbhūmi.

Mouna taba kī kathā bale bujhi,
Artha tāri beḍāi mane khuṁji.
    Caliyā yāo takhan mane bāje,—
    Cini nā āmi, tomāre cini nā je.

❄❄❄

She Who is Many Coloured, 1932

Stranger

I don't know you, not ever,
Hidden you're not, yet you are.
You touch my thoughts for an instant
Like an image and make me jubilant.

Many a days that you did come
Sat with me, yet I was lonesome.
You're to me like a foreigner
Only my sight you did conquer.

Maybe in your mind there's a twinge
Which has kept you veiled with its tinge.
You just stare with a vacant eye,
The forest wafts a long-drawn sigh.

The message in your silence I can find,
It is its meaning I search in my mind.
When you leave then it strikes me again
I don't know you, obscure you remain.

❄ ❄ ❄

Prabhed

Tomāte āmāte āche to prabhed
Jāni tā bandhu, jāni,
Bicched tabu antare nāhi māni.
Ek jyotsnāy jegechi dujane
Sārārāt–jāgā pākhir kujane,
Eki basante dohākār mane
Diyeche āpan bāṇī.

Tumi ceye acha āloker pāne,
Paścāte mor mukh—
Antare tabu gopan milan sukh.
Prabal prabāhe youbana–bān
Bhāsāyeche duṭi dolāita prān,
Nimeṣe dohāre kareche saman
Eki ābarte ṭāni.

Sonār barna mahimā tomār
Biśver manohar,
Āmi abanatapaṇḍur kalebar.
Udās bātāse parān kāṁpāye
Agauraber śaram chāpāye
Āmāre tomār basāila bāṁye
Ekāsane dila āni.
Nabāruna rāg rāṁṅāhaye gela
Kālo bhed rekhākhāni.

❄ ❄ ❄ ❄ ❄

The Distinction

I know, my friend, that between us
There is a distinction,
In my heart I don't accept that separation.
We were awake to the same moon light,
To the songs of the sleepless birds all night
To our minds the same spring alright
Gave its own message of delight.

You are looking at the light,
At your back is my face—
Yet in our hearts is hidden happiness.
The tide of youth in its flooding
Swept away the two hearts floating,
Made them one in a twinkling
In the same current flowing.

Golden colour is your glory
Pleasing to the universe
But pale and demure my look appears.
Languid breeze making hearts shiver
Rising above the shame of disfavour,
Made the two of us sit ever
On the same cushion.
The dark line of distinction
Like the sunrise glow turned crimson.

❄❄❄❄❄

Śeṣ saptak, 1935

No. 6

Diner prānte esechi
Godhulir ghāṭe.
Pathe pathe pātra bharechi
Anek kichu diye.
Bhebechilem cirapather pātheya seguli;
Dām diyechi kaṭhin duḥkhe.
Aṇek karechi saṁgraha mānuṣer kathār hāṭe,
Kichu karechi sañcay premer sadābrate.
Śeṣe bhulechi sārthakatār kathā,
Akārane kuḍiye beḍānoi hayeche andha abhāyāse bāṁdhā;
Phuṭo jhuliṭār śūnya bharbār janye
Biśrām chila nā.
Āj sāmne yakhan dekhi
Phuriye ela path,
Patheyer artha ār raila nā kichui.
Ye pradīp jvalechila milan–śajyār pāśe
Sei pradip enechilem hāte kare.
Tār śikhā nibla āj,
Seṭā bhāsiye dite habe srote.
Sāmner ākāśe jvalbe eklā sandhyār tārā.
Ye bāṁśi bājiyechi
Bhorer āloy, niśīther andhakāre,
Tār śeṣ surṭi beje thāmbe
Rāter śeṣ prahare.

Tār pare?
Ye jībane ālo nibla,
Sur thāmla,
Se ye ei ājker samasta kichur matoi
Bharā satya chila,

The Last Octave, 1935

No. 6

I've come to the end of my day,
to the twilight's shore.
On the way I filled my satchel
with many things.
I thought they were the outlay for the journey eternal
which were paid dearly with intense sorrow.
Gathered much from what others said,
stored some from never ending pursuit of love.
At the end I forgot about fulfillment.
Amassing for its own sake became a blind habit.
In the pursuit of filling the empty satchel with holes
I found no rest.
Today, looking ahead, I see
the end of the road is near
and all the outlays have no value left.
I carried it with me, the lamp
that burnt by the conjugal bed.
Today its flame has been snuffed out
and I must float it in the stream.
The solitary evening star will then glow in the sky.
The flute I played
in the dawn's light— its last tune will end
in the darkness of night,
in the last quarter.

And then?
The life that had its light snuffed out,
its melody stopped,
was as real as everything else
of this day.

Se–kathā ekebārei bhulbe yāni,
Bholāi bhālo.
Tabu tār āge kono ekdiner janya
Keu ekjan
Sei śunyaṭār kāche ekṭā phul rekho
Basanter ye phul ekdin besechi bhālo.

Āmār etadinkār yāoā–āsār pathe
Śukno pātā jhareche,
Sekhāne mileche ālok chāyā,
Briṣṭidhārāy āmkāṁṭhāler ḍāle ḍāle
Jegeche śabder śiharaṇ,
Sekhāne daibe kāro saṅge dekhā hayechila
Jal–bharā ghaṭ niye ye cale giyechila
Cakita pade.

Ei sāmanya chabiṭuku
Ār sab kichu theke beche niye
Keu ekjan āpan dhyāner paṭe eṁko
Kono ekṭi godhūlir dhūsarmuhūrte.

Ār beśi kichu nay.
Āmi ālor premik;
Prānraṅgabhūmite chilum bāṁśi–bājiye.
Pichane phele yāba nā ekṭā nīrab chāyā
Dīrghaniḥśvāser saṅge jaḍiye.

Ye pathik astasūrjyer
Mlāyamān ālor path niyeche
Se to dhulor hāte ujāḍ kare dile
Samasta āpanār dābi;
Sei dhulor udāsīn bedīṭār sāmne
Rekhe yeonā tomār naibedya;
Phire niye yāo anner thāli,

I know you'll totally forget that,
it is better that way.
Yet before that happens, just for a day
someone
please place a flower to that emptiness,
the kind of spring flower I loved once.

Withered leaves had fallen on the trail
I travelled so long.
Light and shadow had met there.
The thrill of the sound of pattering rain had run
through the branches of mango and jack-fruit trees.
By chance there I met someone
who passed with startled steps
with her pitcher full of water.

Choosing this trifling picture from the rest,
someone please
paint it on the canvas of your reflection
in a gray moment of the dusk.

Nothing more I want.
I'm a lover of light.

On the stage of life I played the flute.
I won't leave behind a silent shadow
twined with a deep-drawn sigh.

The traveller who is going the way
of the fading light of the setting sun
has given all his claims
to the dust of the dusk.
Don't leave your offering in front
of the indifferent altar of that dust.
Take back the plate of food
where hunger is staring,

Yekhāne tākiye āche kṣudhā,
Yekhāne atithi base āche dvāre,
Yekhāne prahare prahare bājche ghanṭā
Jibanprabāher saṅge kālaprabāher
Miler mātrā rekhe.

❄ ❄ ❄

No. 34

Pathik āmi.
Path calte calte dekhechi
Purān,e kīrtita kata deś āj kīrti–niḥsva.
Dekhechi darpoddhata pratāper
Abamānita bhagnaśeṣ,
Tār bijay niśān
Bajrāghāte haṭhat stabdha aṭṭahāsir mato
Geche uḍe;
Birāt ahaṁkār
Hayeche sāṣṭāṅge dhulāy pranata,
Sei dhulār pare sandhyābelāy
Bhikṣuk tār jīrna kāṁthā mele base,
Pathiker śranta pad
Sei dhulāy phele cinha,—
Asaṁkhyer nitya padapāte
Se ciṇha yāy lupta haye.

Dekhechi sudur yugāntar
Bālur stare pracchanna,
Yena haṭhat jhañhjār jhāpṭā lege
Kon mahātari
Haṭhat ḍubla dhūsar samudratale,
Sakal āśā niye, gān niye, smṛti niye.

where a guest is waiting by the door,
    where the bells chimes every hour,
keeping its beat with the rhythm of life
    and the flow of time.

❄ ❄ ❄

No. 34

I am a traveller.
  While travelling I've seen
    that countries glorified in legends
      are without any glory today.
I've seen shamed ruins
  of the prowess of bloated pride,
its victory banner blown away
  like loud laughter suddenly muted
                by striking thunder.
Himalayan pride
  prostrate in dust.
In the evening a beggar sits on his
  tattered blanket on that dust.
    The tired feet of travellers
        leave their foot-prints on that dust,
to be wiped out by
    the feet of countless others.

I've seen the ages long past
  buried in layers of sand
as if with the blow of a sudden cyclone
      a giant ship
  suddenly sank in the dark ocean floor
    with all hopes, all songs, all memories.

Ei anityer mājhkān diye calte calte
Anubhab kari āmār hṛtspandane
Asīmer stabdhatā.

❄❄❄

No. 35

Aṅger bāṃdhane bāṁdhāpaḍā āmār prāṇ
Ākasmik cetanār nibiḍatāy
Cañcal haye oṭhe kṣane kṣane,
Takhan kon kathā jānāte tār eta adhairya.
—Ye kathā deher atīt.

Khāṁcār pākhir kaṇṭhe ye bāṇī
Se to kebal khāṁcāri nay,
Tār madhye gopane āche sudur agocarer aranya–marmar,
Āche karuṇ bismṛti.

Sāmne tākiye cokher dekhā dekhi—
E to kebali dekhār jāl–bonā nay.—
Basundharā tākiye thāken nirnimeṣe
Deṣ–pārāno kon deśer dike,
Digbalayer ingitlin
Kon kalpaloker adṛśya saṅkete.

Dirghapath bhālomanday bikīrṇa,
Rātridiner yātrā duḥkhasukher bandhur pathe.
Sudhu kebal path calātei ki e pather lakṣya?

Bhiḍer kalarab periye āsche gāner ahvān,
Tār satya milbe konkhāne?

While travelling through this ephemeral
in my heart-beat I feel
the silence of the eternal.

❄❄❄

No. 35

Encased within my body is my soul.
With some sudden intimate awareness
at times it becomes restless,
at that time which, message it is impatient to tell—
It is the message beyond the body.

The message that is in the voice of a caged bird
is not merely of the cage.
Hidden in it is the murmur of the unknown distant forest,
the sad forgotten memory.

When I look ahead I see with my eyes—
it is not merely weaving a net with sight.
The world gazes without blinking
at a land beyond the lands
hidden in the beckoning of the horizon
in some fairyland's unseen gesture.

A long road is strewn with good and bad.
A journey of night and day is
through the rough road of joy and sorrow.
Is walking on the road the only goal?

Where can you find the truth
of the song that comes
from beyond the clamour of the crowd?

Mātir talāy supta āche bīj.
Tāke sparśa kare caitrer tāp,
Māgher him, śrabaner briṣṭidhārā.
Andhakāre se dekheche abhābiter svapna.
Svapnei ki tār śeṣ?
Uṣār āloy tār phuler prakāś;
Āj nei, tāi bale ki nei konadini?

❄ ❄ ❄

No. 36

Śiter roddur.
Sonā–meśā sabujer ḍheu
Stambhita haye āche segun bane.
Begni–chāyay chomā–lāgā
Jhuri–nāmā bṛddha baṭ
Dāl meleche rāstār o pār paryanta.
Phalsāgācher jharā pātā
Haṭhat hāoāy camke beḍāy uḍe
Dhulor sāṅāt haye.

Kāj–bholā ei din
Udhāo balākār mato
Lin haye caleche niḥsim nilimāy.
Jhāugācher marmardhvanite miśe
Maner madhye ei kathāṭi uṭhche beje,
"Ami āchi."

Kuotalār kāche
Sāmānya oi āmgāch;
Sārā bachar o thāke ātmabismṛta,
Baner sādhāran sabujer abarane

The seed sleeps in the soil.
It is touched by the summer's heat,
winter's dewdrops, water of the rainy season.
In the darkness it dreams of the unthinkable.
Is its end in its dream?
Its flowers manifest with dawn's light.
Just because something is not here today,
does it mean that it never was?

❄ ❄ ❄

No. 36

Sunshine of the winter.
Waves of green blended with gold
are frozen in the teakwood forest.
The old *peepul*-tree with a hint of purple shadow
and its hanging roots has spread its branches
to the other side of the road.
The fallen leaves of the berry trees
are blowing in the wind as chums
of dusts in the sudden gusts of wind.

This day of forgetting work,
like the flying geese
is fading into the endless blue of the sky.
Melting into the murmur of the tamarisk tree.
Only this is sounding in my mind;
"I am."

By the well
is the modest mango tree;
she is self-absorbed all through the year,
blended with the ordinary
green of the forest.

O thāke dhākā.
Eman samay māgher śeṣe
Haṭhat māṭir nīce
Śikaḍe śikaḍe tār śihar lāge,
Śākhāy śākhāy mukulita haye oṭhe bāṇī,
"Āmi āchi."
Candrasūryer ālo āpan bhāṣāy
Svīkār kare tār sei bhāsā.

Alas maner śiyare dāṁḍiye
Hāsen antaryāmī,
Haṭhat den ṭhekiye sonār kāṭhi
Priyār mugdha cokher driṣṭi diye,
Kabir gāner sur diye,
Takhan ye–āmi dhulidhūsar sāmānya dingulir
Madhye miliye chila,
Se dekhā deya ek nimeṣer asāmānya āloke.
Se–sab durmūlya nimeṣ
Kono ratnabhāndāre theke yāy ki nā jānine;
Eiṭku jāni—
Tārā eseche āmār ātmabismṛtir madhye,
Jagiyeche āmār marme
Biśvamarmer nityakāler sei bāni
"Āmi āchi."

❄❄❄

No. 39

Orā ese āmāke bale,
Kabi, mṛtyur kathā śunte cāi tomār mukhe.
Āmi bali,
Mṛtyu ye āmār antaraṅga,
Jaḍiye āche āmār deher sakal tantu.
Tār chanda āmār hṛtspandane,

At the end of the month of *Magh*
in its roots under the soil, rises a shiver
and in her branches blossoms the message,
"I am."
The sun and the moon, in their own language
concur with that message.

Standing at the apex of the idle mind
laughs the One within.
Suddenly He gives the touch of his golden wand
with the beguiled look of a lover,
with the tune of the poet's song.
The "I" that was hidden
in the ordinary dusty days
manifests in a trice in an uncommon light.
I don't know if these priceless moments
are stored in some treasure-chest,
but I know this much—
they have appeared in my self-absorption,
awakening in my soul
the eternal message of the universal soul:
"I am."

❄❄❄

No. 39

They come to me and say,
"Poet, we want to hear about death in your voice."
I say,
"Death is intimate to me,
twined with every fibre of my body.
Its rhythm is in my heart throbs,
its ecstasy swirls in my blood."

Āmār rakte tār ānander prabāha.
Balche se, —calo, calo,
Calo bojhā phelte phelte,
Calo marte marte nimeṣe nimeṣe
Āmāri ṭāne āmāri bege.
Balche, cup kare basa yadi
Yā–kichu āche samastake āṁkḍiye dhare
Tabe dekhbe, tomār jagate
Phul gela bāsi haye,
Pāk dekhā dila ṣukno nadīte,
Mlān hala tomār tārār ālo.
Balche, "themo nā, themo nā,
Pichane phire tākio nā,
Periye yāo puronoke jīrnake klantake acalke.
"Āmi mṛtyu rākhāl
Sṛṣṭike cariye cariye niye calechi
Yug hate yugāntare
Naba naba cāraṇ–kṣetre.

"Yakhan baila jībaner dhārā
Āmi esechi tār pichane pichane,
Deini tāke kono garte āṭak thākte.
Tirer bāṁdhan kāṭiye kāṭiye
Ḍāk diye niye gechi mahāsamudre,
Se samudra āmiyi.

"Bartamān cāy bartiye thākte.
Se cāpāte cāy
Tār sab bojhā tomār māthāy,
Bartamān gile phelte cāy

Death says, "March forward,
go, shedding your burdens,
move on while dying every moment
with my flow, with my impulse."
He also says, "If you are unmoving,
clutching on to all you have,
you'll find that in your world
flowers have faded,
silt has filled your dry riverbeds
and sullied is your stars' light."
He is saying, "Don't stop, don't stop,
don't look back,
go past the old, worn out, tired and the reposed.
I'm the shepherd of death
tending the creation
through the ages
in ever new meadows.

"When life-stream started flowing
I just followed it,
didn't let it get stuck in any hole.
Ever freeing it from the bonds of banks
I've called it to the endless ocean.
I am that ocean.

"The present wants to be.
It wants to load its entire burden
on your shoulder.
The present wants to swallow
your all in its stomach.

Tomār sab–kichu āpan jaṭhare.
Tārpare abical thākte cāy
Ākaṇṭhapūrṇa dānaber mato
Jagaranhin nidrāy.
Takei bale pralay.
Ei ananta acañcal bartamāner hāt theke
Āmi sṛṣṭike paritrāṇ karte esechi,
Antahin naba naba anāgate."

❄❄❄❄❄

Then it wants to remain ever reposed
like a grotesque monster that has its fill
in wake-less sleep.
That's called dissolution.
I've come to save the creation from the clasp
of this ever reposed present
to endless new becoming."

❄ ❄ ❄ ❄ ❄

Patraput, 1936

No. 3

Āj āmār praṇati grahan karo, pṛthibī,
Śeṣ namaskāre abanata dinabsāner beditale.

Mahābīryabatī, tumi bīrabhogyā,
Biparīt tumi lalite kaṭhore,
Miśrita tomār prakṛti puruṣe narīte;
Manuṣer jīban dolāita kara tumi duḥsaha dvande.
Ḍān hāte pūrna kara sudhā
Bām hāte cūrṇa kara pātra,
Tomār lilākṣetra mukharita kara aṭṭabidrūpe;
Duḥsadhya kara bīrer jībaṇke mahātjībane yār adhikār.
Śreyake kara durmūlya,
Kṛpā kara nā kṛpāpatrake.
Tomār gāche gāche pracchanna rekhecha prati muhūrter saṁgrām,
Phale śasye tār jaymālya hay sārthak.
Jale stale tomār kṣamāhin ranarangabhumi,
Sekhāne mṛtyur mukhe ghoṣita hay bijayī prāṇer jayabārtā.
Tomār nirdayatār bhittite uṭheche sabhyatār jayatoraṇ,
Truṭi ghaṭle tār purna mulya sodh hay bināśe.

Tomār itihāser ādi parbe dānaber pratāp chila durjay.
Se pauruṣ, se barbar, se mūḍh.
Tār aṅguli chila sthula, kalākauśal barjita;
Gadā–hāte muṣal–hāte landabhanda kareche se samudra parbat;
Agnite bāṣpete duḥsvapna ghuliye tuleche ākāśe.
Jaḍarājatve se chila ekādhipati,
Prāner pare chila tār andha irṣā.

Plate Made from Leaves, 1936

No. 3

Accept my salutation, Earth, my last homage
bowed at the altar of the setting sun.

You are great in prowess, only to be enjoyed by the mighty.
You counterpoise sweetness and harshness,
your nature is a blend of male and female.
You sway human lives with intolerable conflict.
With your right hand you fill the cup with nectar
and smash it with your left.
Your playground resounds with your mocking laughter.
You make hero's life, which has the right to greatness, hard to attain.
You demand high price for excellence
and show no mercy to those who deserve your mercy.
In your plants hidden is the struggle of every moment,
their crops and fruits are the rewards of victory of this struggle.
Your unforgiving battleground is land and sea
where in the face of death triumphant life declares its victory.
On your mercilessness is the foundation of victory monuments of civilisation.
Destruction is the full price paid for any deficiency.

In the first chapter of your history the Demons ruled unbeaten.
They were masculine, barbaric and ignorant.
Their fingers were gross without any artistic skill.
With their maces and mallets they brought havoc from mountain to sea.
With fire and smoke they churned the sky into nightmare.
They dominated the inanimate world
and they had blind hatred of life.

Debatā elen parayuge—
Mantra paḍlen dānab damaner,
Jaḍer ouddhatya hala abhibhūta;
Jībadhātrī baslen śyamal āstaraṇ pete.
Ūṣhā dāḍālen pūrbācaler śikharcūḍāy,
Paścimsāgartīre sandhyā namlen māthāy niye śāntighaṭ.

Namra hala śikale–bāṁdhā dānab,
Tabu sei ādim barbar āṁkḍe raila tomār itihās.
Byabasthār madhye se haṭhat āne biśrinkhalātā,
Tomār svabhāber kālo garta theke
Haṭhat beḍiye āse eṁkebeṁke.
Tomār nāḍīte lege āche tār pāglāmi.
Debatār mantra uṭhche ākāśe bātāse aranye
Dine rātre
Udātta anudātta mandrasvare.
Tabu tomār bakṣer pātāl theke ādhpoṣā nagdānab
Kṣaṇe kṣaṇe uṭhche phanā tule,
Tār taḍanāy tomār āpan jībke karcha āghāt,
Chārkhār karcha āpan sṛṣṭike.

Śubhe aśubhe sthāpita tomār pādapīṭhe,
Tomār pracanda sundar mahimār uddeśe
Āj rekhe yāba āmār kṣataciṇhalāṇchita jībaner praṇati.
Birāṭ prāṇer, birāt mṛtyur guptasañcār
Tomār ye mātir talāy
Tāke āj sparśa kari, upalabdhi kari sarba dehe mane.
Aganita yugyugāntarer
Asaṁkhya mānuṣer lupta deha puñjita tār dhulāy.
Āmio rekhe yāba kay muṣṭhi dhūli
Āmār samasta sukhduḥkher śeṣ pariṇām,
Rekhe yāba ei nāmagrasī, ākārgrasī, sakal–paricay–grasī
Niḥśabda mahādhūlirāśir madhye.

Gods came in the next age.
With their spell they subdued the Demons
and the insolence of gross matter crumbled.
Mother Earth spread her green cover.
Dawn stood on the eastern mountain peaks.
Evening descended on the western seashore
showering peace from her chalice.

The chained Demons were humbled,
but primal barbarism kept its grip on your history.
Suddenly it brings chaos in order.
From the dark recess of your being
suddenly it comes out with serpentine movement.
Its madness is in your veins.
The spells of gods ring through the sky, wind and forests,
sing day and night, high and low.
Yet from the depth of your body the half-tamed Demons
raise their serpent-hoods.
Their pressure makes you hurt your own creatures
and destroy your own creation.

At your altar mounted on good and evil,
to your stupendous beauty and glory
I offer today my scarred and bruised life's salutation.
Today I feel with my body and mind
the secret movement of vast life and death
beneath your surface.
The remains of countless generations of men
from countless ages
lie buried in your dust.
I too will leave a few handful of dust,
the ultimate measure of all my joys and sorrows:
Add them to that name, form, and fame annihilating
vast, silent heap of dust.

Acal abarodhe abaddha pṛthibī, meghaloke udhāo pṛthibī,
Giriśṛṅgamālār mahat moune dhyānanimagnā pṛthibī,
Nilāmburāśir atandrataraṅge kalamandra mukharā pṛthibī,
Annapūrṇā tumi sundari, annariktā tumi bhīṣanā.
Ek dike āpakkadhanyabhāranamra tomār śaṣyaksetra,
Sekhāne prasanna prabhātsūrya pratidin muche neya śiśirbindu
Kiraṇ uttarīya buliye diye.
Astagāmī sūrya śyāmaśaṣyahillole rekhe yāy akathita ei bāṇī–
'Āmi anandita'.
Anya dike tomār jalahīn phalahīn ātankapāndur marukṣetre
Parikīrṇa paśukankāler madhye marīcikār pretanṛtya.
Baisākhe dekhechi bidyutcancubiddha digantake chiniye nite ela
Kālo śyenpākhir mato tomār jhaḍ,
Samasta ākāśṭā ḍeke uṭhla yena keśar–pholā siṁha,
Tār lejer jhāpaṭe ḍālpālā āluthālu kare
Hatāś banaspati dhulāy paḍla ubuḍ haye.
Hāoār mukhe chuṭla kuḍer cāl
Śikal cheṁḍā kayedi–ḍākāter mato.
Ābār phālgune dekhechi tomār ātapta daksine hāoā
Chaḍiye diyeche birahamilaner svagatapralāp
Āmramukuler gandhe.
Cāṁder peyālā chāpiye diye upciye paḍeche
Svargīya mader phenā.
Baner marmardhvani bātāser spardhāy dhairya hāriyeche
Akasmat kallolacchvāse.

Snigdha tumi, hiṁsra tumi, purātanī, tumi nityanabīnā,
Anādi sṛṣṭir yagñāhutāgni theke beriye esechile
Saṁkhyāgananār atīta pratyuṣe,
Tomār cakratīrther pathe pathe chaḍiye esecha
Śataśata bhāgnā itihāser arthalupta abaśeṣ—
Binā bedanāy bichiye esecha tomār barjita sṛṣṭi
Aganya bismṛtir stare stare.

Earth, besieged by immovable rocks or vanishing into the clouds,
rapt in meditation in the sublime silence of a ring of mountains,
or clamorous with roar of sleepless waves of oceans,
you are beauty and abundance, famine and terror.
On the one hand, endless fields of green crops bent with bounty,
each day wiped free of dew by the gracious morning sun
with its delicate beams.
In the rippling greenness the setting sun leaves this message,
"I am delighted."
On the other hand, in your dry, barren, terrifying deserts is
the ghostly dance of mirage amid strewn animal skeletons.

I have seen your *Baiśākh*-storm swoop like black hawks
ripping the horizon wounded with lightning beaks.
The whole sky roaring like a raging lion with puffed up mane,
whipping trees with its lashing tail
till they crush to the dust in despair.
Thatched roofs breaking loose, blowing in the wind
Like broken-chain convicts.
Again in *Phalgun* I have watched your warm south breeze
spread the raving soliloquies of lovers' union-separation
in the fragrance of mango-blossom.
I've seen the foaming wine of heaven overflowing
from the moon's goblet;
heard low forest-murmur loosing patience with wind's impudence
and suddenly burst into uncontrolled rustling.

You're gentle, you're fierce, you're ancient, you're ever new;
you came out from the sacrificial fire of creation
In a dawn of immeasurably long ago.
Your cyclic path of pilgrimage is littered with
remnants of hundreds of obsolete histories.
You abandon your creation without regret
and leave it in countless layer upon layer—-
all forgotten.

Jībapālinī, āmāder puṣecha
Tomār khaṇḍakāler choṭo choṭo piñjare.
Tāri madhye sab khelār sīmā,
Sab kirtir abasān.

Āj āmi kono moha niye āsi ni tomār sammukhe,
Etadin ye dinrātrir mālā geṁthechi base base
Tār janye amaratār dābi karba nā tomār dvāre.
Tomār ajut nijut batsar sūryapradaksiṇer pathe
Ye bipul nimeṣguli unmīlita nimīlita hate thāke
Tāri ek kṣudra aṁśe kono ekṭi āsaner
Satyamūlya yadi diye thāki,
Jībaner kono ekṭi phalabān khaṇḍake
Yadi jay kare thāki param duḥkhe
Tabe diyo tomār māṭir phoṁṭār ekṭi tilak āmār kapāle;
Se ciṇha yābe miliye
Ye rātre sakal ciṇha parama aciner madhye yāy miśe.
He udāsīn pṛthibī,
Āmāke sampurṇa bholbār āge
Tomār nirmam padaprānte
Āj rekhe yāi āmār praṇati.

*****

Guardian of Life, you nurture us
in tiny cages of fragmented time,
boundaries of all our plays
and limits of all our achievements and fame.

Today I stand before you with no illusion:
I will not demand immortality at your door
for the garland of many days and nights I've woven for you.
In the wake of your circumambulation of the sun
where endless moments open and close like blinks of eternity's eyes;
If I have given true value
to my little place in a tiny fragment of time
if I've won a scrap of success
with supreme pain,
then mark my forehead with a dot made from your clay—
to be wiped out in the night
when all marks fade into the supreme unknown.
O indifferent Earth,
before I am utterly forgotten
let me offer at your ruthless feet
my salutation.

❄ ❄ ❄ ❄ ❄

Śyāmalī, 1936

Bāṁśioālā

"Ogo bāṁśioālā,
Bājāo tomār bāṁśi,
Śuni āmār nutan nām"
—Ei bale tomāke pratham ciṭhi likhechi,
Mane ache to?
Āmi tomār baṁlādeśer meye.
Sṛṣṭikartā puro samay den ni
Āmāke mānuṣ kare gaḍte,—
Rekhechen ādhāādhi kare.
Antare bāhire mil hay ni
Sekāle ār ājker kāle,
Mil hay ni byathāy ār buddhite,
Mil hay ni śaktite ār icchāy.
Āmāke tule den ni e yuger pārāni noukoy,
Calā āṭak kare phele rekhechen
Kālasroter o pāre bāludāṅāy.
Sekhān theke dekhi
Prakhar āloy jhāpsā dūrer jagat,—
Binā kārane kāṅāl man adhīr haye oṭhe,
Dui hāt bāḍiye dei,
Nāgāl pāi ne kichui kono dike.
Belā to kāṭe nā,
Base thāki joār–jaler dike ceye—
Bhese yāy mukti–pārer kheyā,
Bhese yāy dhanapatir diṅā,
Bhese yāy calti belār ālochāyā.
Eman samay bāje tomār bāṁśi
Bharā jībaner sure.
Marā diner nāḍir madhey
Dabdabiye phire āse prāṇer beg.

She Who is Dark, 1936

The Flute Player

"Oh, Flute-player,
please play your flute.
Let me hear my new name."
Thus I wrote my first letter,
do you remember it?
I am a girl from your Bengal.
The creator did not spend the time
needed to make me a complete person.
He left me half done.
So there is no harmony between my heart within and without,
and the age long past and the present.
There is no concord between my pain and intellect
and no balance between my will and desire.
He did not put me in a modern ferryboat.
He stopped my journey and left me stuck
in the sandbank on the other side of the flow of time.
From there I see
the distant world blurred in blinding light.
For no reason, my thirsty mind becomes restless.
I stretch out my two arms
but can't touch anything anywhere.
My time does not pass.
I sit gazing at the water in high tide where
floats away the ferryboat to the land of free,
floats away the wealthy merchant's boat and
floats away the light and shadow of the present.
At such a time your flute plays
the tune of a fulfilled life.
In my dead life's veins
life force surges back throbbing.

Ki bājāo tumi,
Jāni ne se sur jāgāy kār mane ki byathā.
Bujhi bājāo pañcamrāge
Dakṣiṇ hāoār nabayoubaner bhāṭiāri.
Śunte śunte nijeke mane hay—
Ye chila pahaḍtalir jhirjhire nadī,
Tār buke haṭhat uṭheche ghaniye
Śrābaner badalrātri.
Sakāle uṭhe dekhā yāy pāḍi geche bhese,
Ekgumye pātharguloke ṭhelā dicche
Asahya sroter ghurṇi–mātan.

Āmār rakte niye āse tomār sur—
Jhaḍer ḍāk, banyār ḍāk, āguner ḍāk,
Pāṁjarer upare āchāḍ–khāoā
Maraṇ–sāgarer ḍāk,
Gharer śikal–nāḍā udāsī hāoār ḍāk.
Yena hāṁk diye āse
Apūrner sankīrṇa khāde
Pūrṇa sroter ḍākāti,
Chiniye nebe bhāsiye nebe bujhi.
Aṅge aṅge pak diye oṭhe
Kālbaiśākhīr ghurni–mār–khāoā
Araṇyer bakuni.

Ḍānā dey ni bidhātā,
Tomār gān diyeche āmār svapne
Jhoḍo ākāśe uḍo praṇer pāglāmi.
Ghare kāj kari śānta haye;
Sabāi bale 'bhālo'.
Tārā dekhe āmār icchār nei jor,
Sāḍā nei lobher,
Jhāpaṭ lāge māthār upar,
Dhuloy luṭoi māthā.

I don't know what you play
or what pain the tune evokes in whose mind.
Perhaps you play in cuckoo's note
the decline of the youthful south breeze.
While listening to it I think of myself
as a gently flowing stream at the feet of a mountain,
in whose heart has suddenly come
the rainy night of *Sraban.*
In the morning can be seen the banks flooded,
the unbearable swirl of water
pushing the stubborn stones.

Your tune brings in my blood—
the rumble of storm, the surge of flood, the roar of fire,
the assault of the ocean of death
on the rib-cage,
the stirring of the door-chain by the listless wind.
It brings through the narrow channel of unfulfillment
the boom of high tide's plunder
as if to snatch and sweep me away.
Throughout my being coils up the agony
of a forest battered
by the whirlwind storm of *Baishakh.*

Providence did not give me wings,
but gave me your songs in my dreams—
the madness of a heart flying in a stormy sky.
I do my housework calmly
and everyone says, "Good."
They see that there is no strength in my will,
no response to my desires.
A gust of storm strikes my head
and it rolls in the dust.

Duranta ṭhelāy niṣedher pāhārā kāt kare pheli
Nei eman buker pāṭā;
Kaṭhin kare yāni ne bhālobāste,
Kām̐dte śudhu jāni,
Jāni eliye paḍte pāye.

Bām̐śioālā,
Beje oṭhe tomār bām̐śi,—
Ḍāk paḍe amartyaloke;
Sekhāne āpan garimāy
Upare uṭheche āmār māthā.
Sekhāne kuāśār pardā–chęm̐ḍā
Taruṇ surya āmār jīban.
Sekhāne āguner dānā mele dey
Āmār bāraṇ–na–mānā āgraha,
Uḍe cale ajānā śūnyapathe
Pratham–kṣudhāy–asthir garuḍer mato.
Jege oṭhe bidrohinī.
Tīksna cokher āḍe jānāy ghṛṇā
Cār diker bhīrur bhiḍke,
Kṛśa kuṭiler kāpuruṣatāke.

Bām̐śioālā,
Hayto āmāke dekhte ceyecha tumi.
Jāni ne, ṭhik jāygāṭi kothāy,
Ṭhik samay kakhan,
Cinbe keman kare.
Dosar–hārā āṣāḍher jhillijhanak rātre
Sei nārī to chāyārupe
Geche tomār abhisāre cokh–eḍāno pathe.
Sei ajānāke kata basante
Pariyecha chām̐der mālā,
Śukobe nā tār phul.

I don't have the guts to even bend the barriers
of taboo with one unrestrained blow.
I don't know to love with all my might.
I know only to shed tears,
I know to submit at the feet.

O flute-player,
your flute starts to play
and summons the heaven.
There my head, in its own pride,
Rises high.
There my life is like the rising sun
coming out tearing the curtain of fog.
There my fervour spreads its wings,
defying disapproval,
flies to the unknown emptiness
like *Garuda* bird fretful from its first hunger.
Awakens the rebel in me
and with piercing look shows revulsion
to the crowd of cowards around
and the impotence of the weak-kneed hypocrites.

O flute-player,
perhaps you wanted to meet me.
I don't know which is the right place,
when is the right time,
or how you will recognise me.
In a forlorn *Ashadh* night filled with crickets' chirping,
that woman, like a shadow, has gone for her love-tryst with you,
following the path hidden from the eyes.
You adorned that stranger
with garlands of rhythm in many springs.
Those flowers will never wither.

Tomār ḍāk śune ekdin
Gharpoṣā nirjīb meye
Andhakār kon theke
Beriye ela ghomṭā–khasā narī.
Yena se haṭhat–gāoā natun chanda Balmīkir,
Camak lāgālo tomākei.
Se nāmbe nā gāner āsan theke;
Se likhbe tomāke ciṭhi
Rāginīr ābchāyāy base.
Tumi jānbe nā tār ṭhikānā.

Ogo bāṁśoāla,
Se thāk tomār bāṁśir surer duratve.

❄❄❄❄❄

One day, hearing your summon,
the homebound lifeless girl
came out of her dark corner
as a woman casting away her veil.
As if she was a suddenly-sung new rhyme of *Valmiki*
and she amazed you.
She won't come down from her seat of singing.
She will write you letters
staying in shadow of your melodies.
You will not know her address.

Oh Flute-player,
let her stay at a distance in the melody of your flute.

*****

Prāntik, 1938

No.8

Raṅgamañce eke eke nibe gela yabe dīpaśikhā,
Rikta hala sabhātal, āṁdhārer masī–abalepe
Svapnacchabi–muche–yāoā suṣuptir mato śānta hala
Citta mor niḥśabder tarjanisaṁkete. Etakāl
Ye sāje raciyāchinu āpanār nātyaparicay
Pratham uṭhite yabanikā, sei sāj muhūrtei
Hala nirarthak. Cinhita kariāchinu āpanāre
Nānā cinhe, nānā barnaprasādhane sahasrer kāche,
Muchila tā, apanāte āpanār niguḍha pūrnatā
Āmāre karila stabdha, suryāster antim satkāre
Dinānter śunyatāy dharār bicitra citralekhā
Yakhan pracchanna hay, bādhāmukta ākāś yeman
Nirbāk bismaye stabdha tārādīpta ātmaparicaye.

***

No 18

Naginīrā cāri dike pheliteche biṣākta niśvās,
Śāntir lalit bāṇī sonaibe byartha parihās—
Bidāy nebār āge tāi
Ḍāk diye yāi
Dānaber sāthe yārā saṁgrāmer tare
Prastut hateche ghare ghare.

*****

The Borderland, 1938

No. 8

When the lights on the stage went out one by one,
the theatre becomes empty and as the ink-smear
of darkness of deep sleep covers the images
of dream, so my mind became still at the gesture
of silence. The make–up I carefully wore for my
stage role spending a long time became meaningless
as soon as the curtain rose. The many defining
marks and colours I had put on for appearing
before thousands were all wiped out. My deep
fulfillment silenced me within myself,
as after the sunset the matchless images
of the earth become cloaked in emptiness
and the sky, freed from bonds, become silent
in speechless wonder at the appearance of star light.

❄❄❄

No. 18

Everywhere the serpents' poison-breath manifest
The gentle voice of peace will sound like vain jest.
Before I go therefore,
Those I implore
Who, in their homes, are preparing
To wage war against the evil beings.

❄❄❄❄❄

Rogśayāy, 1940

No. 4

Ajasra diner ālo
Jāni, ekdin
Du caksure diyechile ṛṇ.
Phirāye nebār dābi jānāyecha āj
Tumi, mahārāj.
Śodh kare dite habe jāni,
Tabu kena sandhyādipe
Phela chāyākhāni.
Racile ye ālo diye taba biśvatal
Āmi sethā atithi kebal.
Hethā hothā yadi paḍe thāke
Kono kṣudra phāṁke
Nai hala purā
Seṭuku tukurā—
Rekhe yeo phele
Abahele,
Yethā taba rath
Śeṣ ciṇha rekhe yāy antim dhulāy
Sethāy racite dāo āmār jagat
Alpa kichu ālo thāk,
Alpa kichu cāyā
Ār kichu māyā.
Chāyāpathe lupta āloker pichu
Hayto kuḍāye pābe kichu—
Kaṇāmātra leś
Tomār ṛnner abaśeṣ.

❄❄❄

On the Sick-bed, 1940

No. 4

I know, once to my eyes
You loaned
the endless light of days.
You've come, my Lord,
with the demand to take it back.
I must pay you back, I know
yet why cast your shadow
in the evening lamp?
In your creation of lights
I'm just a guest.
Here and there,
in a little crack as such,
maybe not much,
leave that portion
in Your inattention
where your chariot leaves
its last trace in the last dust.
There you let me build my world.
Let there be a little light,
a little shadow
and a little tenderness.
In the shadowy path, in the wake of your light
maybe you will sight
a sprinkling
of your debt's balance remaining.

❄ ❄ ❄

No. 26

Āmār kīrtire āmi kari nā biśvās.
Jāni, kālasindhu tāre
Niyata tarangāghāte
Dine dine dibe lupta kari.
Āmār biśvās āpanāre.
Dui belā sei pātra bhari
E biśver nityasudhā
Kariyāchi pān.
Prati muhūrter bhālobāsā
Tār mājhe hayeche sañcita.
Duḥkhabhāre dīrṇa kare nāi,
Kālo kare nai dhūli
Śilpere tāhār.
Āmi jāni, yāba yabe
Saṁsārer raṅgabhūmi chāḍi,
Sakṣya debe puṣpaban ṛtute ṛtute
E biśvere bhālobāsiyāchi.
E bhālobāsāi satya, e janmer dān.
Bidāy nebār kāle
E satya amlān haye mrityure karibe asvīkār.

***

No. 37

Dhūsar godhūlilagne sahasā dekhinu ekdin
Mṛtyur dakṣiṇ bāhu jībaner kaṇṭhe bijaḍita,
Rakta sūtragāchi diye bāṁdhā;
Cinilām takhani doṁhāre.
Dekhilām niteche youtuk
Barer caram dān maraner badhū;
Daksinbāhute bahi caliyāche yugānter pāne.

*****

No. 26

In my deeds I don't believe.
I know the ocean of time,
striking with its waves, day by day
will relegate them to oblivion.
In myself I do believe.
Filling its chalice
twice a day I drank
this world's eternal nectar.
The love of every moment
was collected there.
The weight of sorrow
didn't break it, dust didn't
sully its splendour.
I know, when
I'll leave this world's stage,
the flower garden, season after season
will bear witness to my love for this world.
This love is the truth, this life's offering.
At the time of my parting
This truth, becoming untarnished, will disavow death.

❄❄❄

No. 37

In the gray twilight hour suddenly I saw one day
That Death's right arm folded around Life's neck.
At that moment I recognised the two
Twined with a blood red thread.
I saw Death's bride with the dowry of
Supreme sacrifice for the groom;
In her right hand going towards the endless time.

❄❄❄❄❄

Nabajātak, 1940

Hindusthān

More Hindusthān
Bārbār kareche āhvān
Kon śiśukāl hate paścimdiganta–pāne,
Bhārater bhāgya yethā nṛtyalilā kareche śmaśāne,
Kāle kāle
Taṇḍaber tāle tāle,
Dillite Āgrāte
Mañjirjhankār ār dur śakunir dvani–sāthe;
Kāler manthandaṇḍāghāte
Ucchali uṭheche yethā pātharer phenastupe
Adriṣter aṭṭahāsya abhrabhedī prāsāder rūpe.
Lakṣmi–alakṣmir dui biparīt pathe
Rathe pratirathe
Dhūlite dhūlite yethā pāke pāke kareche racanā
Jaṭil rekhār jāle śubha–aśubher ālpanā.
Naba naba dhvajā hāte naba naba sainikbāhinī
Ek kāhinīr sūtra chinna kari ārek kāhinī
Bāraṁgbār granthi diye kareche yojan.
Prānganprācīr yār akasmāt kareche laṅghan
Dasyudal,
Ardharātre dvār bheṅe jagiyeche ārta kolāhal,
Kareche āsan–kāḍākāḍi,
Kṣudhiter annathāli niyeche ujāḍi.
Rātrire bhulila tārā oiśvaryer maśāl–āloy—
Piḍīta pīḍankārī doṁhe mili sādāy kāloy
Yekhāne raciyāchila dyūtakhelāghar,

The Newly Born, 1940

Hindustan

From my childhood that is long gone
Hindustan has sent me summons
Again and again to its western gate
Where through the ages India's fate
Had always danced in the ground of cremation,
In Delhi, Agra the dance of destruction
With anklets' jingling. Distant vultures' cry
With the churning of time, rose to the sky.
Marbles piled upon marbles pierced the sky as palaces, fortress—
The mocking thunderous laughter of fortune's excess.
Where fortune and misfortune opposing
The clouds of dusts swirling
From opposing chariots did design
A tracery of good and evil in entangled lines.
Again and again new armies under new banners
Sliced the threads of one episode and joined with another.
In the dead of night, the invading marauders
Crossing someone's courtyard border,
Broke down the doors to seize his territory,
Raised clamour of terror and emptied the granary.
With the glow of their riches
They ignored the night's darkness.
Where the oppressor and the oppressed made a place
In black and white for playing chess
Today at last

Abaśeṣe sethā āj ekmātra birāt kabar
Prānta hate prānte prasārita;
Sethā jayī ār parājita
Ekatre kareche abasān
Bahu śatābdīr yata mān asammān.
Bhagnajānu pratāper chāyā sethā śīrṇa yamunāy
Preter āhvān bahi cali yāy
Bale yāy—
Āro chāyā ghanāiyeche astadiganter
Jīrṇa yugānter.

❄ ❄ ❄ ❄ ❄

Lies from one end to the other a vast
Graveyard. The vanquished and the victor
Together ended centuries of shame and splendour.
The shadow of the broken down invincible power
Now floats away on the lean Yamuna, carrying the call of spectre
And say—-
More shadows of ages of decay
Are gathering
In the horizon at the time of the sun setting.

❄ ❄ ❄ ❄ ❄

Ārogya, 1941

No. 6

Ati dūre ākāśer sukumār pāndur nilimā.
Araṇya tāhāri tale ūrdhve bāhu meli
Āpan śyāmal arghya niḥśabde kariche nibedan.
Megher taruṇ roudra dharaṇīr pare
Bicāyila dike dike saccha āloker uttarīya.
E kathā rahinu likhe
Udāsīn citrkar ei chabi muchibār āge.

❄ ❄ ❄

No. 8

Ekā base saṁsārer prānta jānālāy
Diganter nīlimāy cokhe paḍe ananter bhāṣā.
Ālo āse chāyāy jaḍita
Śirīṣer gāch hate śyāmaler snigdha sakhya bahi.
Bāje mane— nahe dūr, nahe bahu dūr.
Patharekhā līn hala astagiriśikhar–āḍāle,
Stabha āmi diganter pānthaśālā dvāre,
Dūre dīpti dey kṣaṇe kṣaṇe
Seṣ tīrthamandirer cūḍā.
Sethā siṁhadvāre bāje din–abasāner rāginī
Yār mūrchanāy meśā e janmer yā–kichu sundar,
Sparśa yā kareche prāṇ dīrgha yātrāpathe
Purnatār ingitj ānāye.
Bāje mane— nahe dūr, nahe bahu dūr.

❄ ❄ ❄

Recovery, 1941

No. 6

Far away is the pale tender blue sky.
The forest below with arms stretched high
is presenting its green offering.
Fresh sunshine of spring
spreads all round its radiant scarf.
This I have recorded
before it is wiped out by the painter disinterested.

❄ ❄ ❄

No. 8

Sitting alone by the world's last window
I see the message of the eternal in the blue-horizon.
Light comes mixed with shadow,
Carrying the refreshing fellowship of the rain-tree.
In my mind I hear – not far, not very far.
Fades the road beyond the setting sun,
Silent I am at the doorstep of the day's-end-inn.
Far away, every now and then, flashes
The crown of the last pilgrim-temple.
There at the main portal plays the melody of day's ending
In whose cadence mingles all that was beautiful in this life,
Which is carrying the hint of fulfillment
Touched my heart through this long journey.
In my mind I hear – not far, not very far.

❄ ❄ ❄

No. 10

Alas samay–dhārā beye
Man cale śunya–pāne ceye.
Se mahāśūnyer pathe chāyā–āṁkā chabi paḍe cokhe.
Katakāl dale dale geche kata loke
Sūdīrgha atīte
Jayoddhata prabal gatite.
Eseche sāmrāyalobhī pāṭhāner dal,
Eseche mogal;
Bijayer rathercākā
Uḍāyeche dhūlujāl, uḍiyāche bijay patākā.
Śūnya pathe cāi,
Āj tār kono ciṇha nāi.
Nirmal se nīlimāy prabhāte o sandhyāy rāṅālo
Yuge yuge śūryoday–śūryāster ālo.
Ābār sei śūnytale
Āsiyāche dale dale
Louhabāṁdhā pathe
Analniḥśvāsī rathe
Prabal iṁgrej,
Bikirṇa kareche tār tej.
Jāni tāro path diye baye yābe kāl,
Kothāy bhāsāye debe sāmrājyer deśbeḍājāl.
Jāni tār paṇyabāhī senā
Jyotiṣkaloker pathe rekhāmātra ciṇha rākhibe nā.
Mātir pṛthibī–pāne aṁkhi meli yabe
Dekhi sethā kala kalarabe
Bipul janatā cale
Nānā pathe nānā dale dale
Yug yugāntar hate mānuṣer nitya prayojane
Jībane marane.
Orā cirakāl
Tāne dāṁḍ, dhare thāke hāl;
Orā māṭhe māṭhe
Bīj bone, pākā dhān kāte.

No. 10

My mind flies gazing at sky's emptiness
With the flow of time's laziness.
In that vast emptiness I see pictures in shadows
Of people, who marched proudly in rows after rows
In times long gone
After victories they won.
With their lust for empire came the *Pathan* tribal,
Came the Mughals.
Dusts from their chariot wheels clouded the sky
And the victory flags flew high.
Searching those empty skyways now
I find no trace of them anyhow.
Through the ages rays of sunrise and sunset
Have coloured the clear blue sky their best.
Again on those empty roads
Have come in hordes
On iron paths, riding
Chariots, fire breathing
The mighty English race,
To declare their prowess.
I know time will pass through yet
Sweeping away their empire's net.
I know also their army, carrying wealth away
Will leave no trace on the cosmic roadway.
When I open my eyes to this earth of clay
I see the vast humanity going everyday
Through the ages,
Following roads to different places.
In bands they zestfully go on their way
To meet life and death's needs of the day.
Forever they row boats, hold helms, seed field
After field, harvest the ripe crops they yield.
They work in cities and on the lands
With their hands.

Orā kāj kare
Nagare prāntare.
Rājchatra bheṅe paḍe, raṇaḍankā śabda nāhi tole,
Jayastambha mūḍhasama artha tār bhole,
Raktamākhā astra hāte yata rakta–āṁkhi
Śisupāṭhya kāhinīte thāke mukh dhāki.
Orā kāj kare
Deśe deśāntare,
Aṅga–baṅga–kaliṅger samudra–nadīr ghāte ghāte,
Punjābe bombāi–gujrāte.
Guruguru garjan gungun svar
Dinrātre gāṁthā paḍi dinayātrā kariche mukhar.
Duḥkha sukh dibasrajanī
Mandrita kariyā tole jībaner mahāmantradhvani.
Śata śata sāmrajyer bhagnāśeṣ–pare
Orā kāj kare.

❄ ❄ ❄ ❄ ❄

Empires crumble, war-drums become silent
Victory monuments, like fools, forget their intent.
With bloodied weapons in hand and blood-shot looks
All victors hide their faces in children's storybooks.
They work in their homeland
And in other lands—
In the towns on the riverbanks and in the ports of call
Of Bihar, Orrisa, the Punjab, Bombay, Gujarat and Bengal.
Days and nights that string day to day living resound
With their clamorous rumble and buzzing sound.
In their joys and sorrows all night and day
Make vibrant the great purpose of life's play.
On the ruins of empires countless
Their work goes on endless.

❄ ❄ ❄ ❄ ❄

Janmadine, 1941

No. 10

Bipulā e pṛthibīr katatuku jāni.
Deśe deśe kata–nā nagar rājdhānī—
Manuṣer kata kīrti, kata nadī giri sindhu maru,
Katā–na ajānā jīb, kata–nā aparicita taru
Raye gela agocare. Biśāl biśver āyojan;
Mor man juḍe thāke ati kṣudra tāri ek koṇ.
Sei kṣobhe paḍi grantha bhramanbrittānta āche yāhe
Akṣay utsāhe—
Yethā pāi citramayī barnanār bāṇī
Kuḍāyiā āni.
Jnāner dīnatā ei āpanār mane
Pūraṇ kariyā lai yata pāri bhikṣālabdha dhane.

Āmi pṛthibīr kabi, yethā tār yata uṭhe dhvani
Āmār bāṁśir sure sāḍā tār jāgibe takhani,
Ei svarasādhanāy pouṁchila nā bahutara ḍāk—
Raye geche phāṁk.
Kalpanāy anumāne dharitrīr maha–ekatān
Kata–nā niśtabdha kṣane pūrna kariyāche mor prāṇ.
Durgam tuṣārgiri asim niḥśabda nilīmāy
Aśruta ye gān gāy
Āmār antare bārbār
Pāthāyeche nimantraṇ tār.
Dakṣinmerur ūrdhe ajñāta ye tārā
Mahājanaśūnyatāy rātri tār kariteche sārā,
Se āmār ardharātre animeṣ cokhe
Anidrā kareche sparśa apurba āloke.
Sudūrer mahāplābī pracaṇḍa nirjhar
Maner gahane mor pāṭhāyāche svar.

On My Birthday, 1941

No. 10

This vast world I hardly know at all.
In many lands are so many cities, so many capitals.
So many deeds of man, so many rivers, mountains, deserts, seas
So many unknown creatures, so many unknown trees,
Remain unseen by me. Of all the vast earth's treasures
My mind is occupied with a paltry measure.
Dissatisfied, books on travel I read
With keen interest indeed—-
Wherever I find pictorial descriptions
I keep in my collection.
The paucity of my awareness I try to fill
With knowledge I beg and steal.

I'm a poet of the earth. When anywhere rises a sound
In the tune of my flute at once it should resound.
There are many lacunas in my striving
As many calls were not in my hearing.
In many moments of silence the earth's grand unison
Filled my heart in my imagination and intuition.
The silent songs, the unreachable snow-covered mountains
In the silence of endless blue song, have again and again
In my heart
Invitations they did impart.
High above the south pole in the endless sky
The nameless star that spends nights with unblinking eye
Halfway through the night
On my sleepless eye cast a beatific light.
To the depth of my mind came the call
From the far away mighty and overflowing waterfall.

Prakṛtir oikyatansrote
Nānā kabi dhāle nānā dik hate;
Tāder sabār sāthe āche mor eimātra yog—
Saṅga pāi sabākār, lābh kari ānander bhog,
Gītabhāratīr āmi pāi to prasād
Nikhiler saṁgiter svād.

Sab ceye durgam–ye mānuṣ āpan antarāle,
Tār kono parimāp nāi bāhirer deśe kāle.
Se antarmay
Antar miśāle tabe tār antarer paricay.
Pāi ne sarbatra tār prabeśer dvār,
Bādhā haye āche mor beḍāguli jibanyātrār.
Cāṣi kṣete cālāiche hāl,
Tāṁti base tāṁt bone, jele phele jāl—
Bahudūrprasārita eder bicitra karmabhār
Tāri pare bhar diye caliteche samasta saṁsār.
Ati kṣudra aṁgśe tār sammāner ciranirbāsane
Samājer ucca mañce basechi saṁkirṇa bātāyane.
Mājhe mājhe gechi āmi opāḍār prāṅgaṇer dhāre,
Bhitare prabeś kari se śakti chila nā ekebāre.
Jībane jībane yog karā
Nā hale kṛtrim panye byartha hay gāner pasarā.
Tāi āmi mene nei se nindār kathā
Āmār surer apūrṇatā.
Āmār kabitā, jāni āmi,
Geleo bicitrapathe hay nāi sarbatragāmī.
Kṛṣāṇer jībaner śarik ye jan,
Karme o kathāy satya ātmīyatā kareche arjan,
Ye āche māṭir kāchākāchi,
Se kabir bāṇi–lāgi kān pete āchi.
Sāhityer ānander bhoje
Nije yā pari nā dite nitya āmi thāki tāri khoṁje.

In the unity of nature's flow, poets from many directions
Blend their songs. With all of them I've this connection:
I enjoy the feast of pleasure,
Their friendship I treasure.
I receive the grace of the goddess of music
And a taste of songs cosmic.

Man within himself is most inaccessible.
In any time or place without, he is unfathomable.
He is in his soul
And can only be known by connecting soul with soul.
I don't find the entrance door everywhere.
My station in life stands as the barrier.
The field, the farmer is ploughing;
The fisherman is casting his net, the weaver is weaving —
Their diverse work spreads far and wide
On them, functioning of the whole world resides.
In a tiny corner, in the ever isolation of fame
In society's crest, seated at a narrow window I remain.
Sometimes I have been to the courtyard of the other side
But never had the courage at all to venture inside.
If between lives there is no connection,
Vain will be wares of songs with imitation.
That is why I respect my critics and admit
That the tunes of my songs are not complete.
I know, though my poems are diverse,
All paths they did not traverse.
The one who is a partner of the cultivator of the land
True unity of words and deeds if he does command,
The poet who is close to the land
To hear his message eagerly I stand.
What I could not give for letters'-fest
To seek that always I rest.

Seṭā satya hok,
Śudhu bhaṅgī diye yena nā bholāy cokh.
Satya mūlya nā diyei sāhityer khyāti karā curi
Bhālo nay, bhālo nay nakal se śoukhin majduri.

Eso kabi akhyātajaner
Nirbāk maner.
Marmer bedanā yata kariyā uddhār—
Prānhīn e deśete gānhīn yethā cāri dhār,
Abajñār tāpe śuṣka nirānanda sei marubhūmi
Rase purṇa kari dāo tumi.
Antare ye utsa tār āche āpanāri
Tāi tumi dāo to udbāri.
Sahityer oikyatansaṁgitsabhāy
Ektārā yāhāder tārāo sammān yena pāy—
Mūk yārā duḥkhe sukhe,
Nataśir stabdha yārā biśver sammukhe,
Ogo guni,
Kāche theke dūre yārā tāhāder bāṇī yena śuni.
Tumi thāko tāhāder jñāti,
Tomār khyātite tārā pāy yena āpanār khyāti—
Āmi bāraṁgbār
Tomāre kariba namaskār.

❄ ❄ ❄ ❄ ❄

Let that be genuine in passion
May it not beguile only with its fashion.
Without paying true price, to steal honour
In letters is not fair. Nor is fair the fake luxury of labour.

Come, the poet of the nameless
And the mind voiceless.
Root out from hearts all suffering.
Fill with glad tidings
This land, all quarters without song and lifeless
And due to extreme scorn turned dry and joyless.
May you free the wellspring
That is in his being.
Let the lowly receive approbation
In the assembly of letters' adulation.
O you laudable, may I hear
The voice of those very far, though they are near,
The afflicted, voiceless, silent
And standing before the world, head bent.
May you be their friend,
With your fame may they also have fame.
I will salute you again and again.

❄❄❄❄❄

Śeṣlekhā, 1941

No. 13

Pratham diner sūrya
Praśna karechila
Sattār nūtan ābirbhābe—
Ke tumi.
Mele ni uttar.
Batsar batsar cale gela,
Dibaser śeṣ surya
Śeṣ praśna uccārila paścimsāgartīre,
Nistabdha sandhāy—
Ke tumi.
Pela nā uttar.

❄ ❄ ❄

No. 15

Tomār sṛṣtir path rekhecha ākirṇa kari
Bicitra chalanājāle,
Hey chalanāmayī.
Mithyā biṣvāser phāṁd petecha nipuṇ hāte
Saral jībane.
Ei prabañcanā diye mahattvere karecha ciṇhita;
Tār tare rākha ni gopan rātri.
Tomār jyotiṣka tāre
Ye–path dekhāy
Se ye tār antarer path,

Last Writings, 1941

No. 13

The first day's sun
questioned with the new stirring
of existence,
"Who are you?"
Found no answer.

Aeons passed.
The day's last sun,
In the evening's silence
asked the last question
from the western seashore,
"Who are you?"
Got no answer.

❄ ❄ ❄

No. 15

Strewn with a net of diverse deception
is the path of your creation,
O you enchantress.
With adept hands you've laid
the snare of false beliefs
in innocent lives.
With this deception you've marked the great;
for him you haven't left night's secret.
The course that your stars
show him
is his inner path,

Se ye cirasvaccha, sahaj biśvāse se ye
Kare tāre cirasamujjval.
Bahire kuṭil hok antare se ṛju,
Ei niye tāhār gourab.
Loke tāre bale biḍambita.
Satyere se pāy
Āpan āloke dhouta antare antare.
Kichute pāre nā tāre prabancite,
Śeṣ puraskār niye yāy se ye
Āpan bhāndare.
Anāyāse ye pereche chalanā sahite
Se pāy tomār hāte
Śantir akṣay adhikār.

❄❄❄❄❄

ever transparent,
ever resplendent
by his simple faith.
However crafty outside, he is simple inside;
that's his pride.
Others say that he has been deceived.
In his heart truth he receives
bathed in his inner light.
Nothing can deceive him;
he takes his last reward
to his own store–house.
Whoever can suffer your trickery at ease,
from your hands he receives
everlasting claim to peace.

❄ ❄ ❄ ❄ ❄

Glossary

Amlaki is a deciduous tree with feathery leaves. It bears a small round sour-astringent fruit which has medicinal value and is also used as a condiment.

Ashadh is the third month of the Bengali calendar, from mid-April to mid-May and first of the two months of the rainy season, mid-June to mid-July.

Baishakh is the first month of the Bengali calendar, from mid-April to mid-May and is the first month of the two month summer season.

Bakul is a small creamy-white star-like flower from large trees and has a strong-sweet scent. The flowers bloom from February to July and drops on the ground by the morning, making a carpet of flowers. It is often praised in Bengali poetry.

Bharat or *Bharatbarsa* is the name of India from the ancient times.

Brahmini duck is the name of the handsome bird *Casaroa rutila* or 'Ruddy Shieldrake'. It is frequently seen on the sandy shores of the rivers of the Gangetic plain in pairs but always at some distance apart and lends to common comparison in literature for faithful lovers and spouses. A Hindu legend is that two lovers for their indiscretion were transformed into Brahmini ducks and were condemned to pass the night apart from each other and on the opposite banks of the river. All night long each, in its turn, asks its mate if it shall come across but the response is always 'no'.

Champak (Michelia champa) is an evergreen tree bearing yellow-orange flowers with heavy fragrance.

Ganesha is the son of Shiva and Parvati and is worshipped first in all Hindu rituals. He is the deity for success in all endeavours of man.

Gaudsarang is one of the ragas or moods in Indian classical music.

Ghat is a landing place, a path of descent to a river or a pond, the place of a ferry and also a quay.

Indra is the mythological king of the gods.

Koel is the name of a bird belonging to the cuckoo family. It is the Indian nightingale and devotes best part of the night to vocal exercise as the nightingale.

Kush is a variety of grass with sharp points. It is used in rituals.

Magh is the tenth month of the Bengali calendar from mid-January to mid-February and the second month of the two-month winter season.

Mandakini is the river Ganges when it flows through the mythological heavenly world.

Mandar is *palte madar* with its scarlet blossoms. But in this poem it is clearly the mythological *mandar*, which is a celestial tree growing in the pleasure gardens of the gods.

Menaka is a celestial nymph and a dancer in Indra's court.

Nandan is the heavenly pleasure garden of Indra. It is always pleasant like spring time there.

Palash is a kind of red flower having no fragrance of its tree. The flowers blossom on leafless branches in the spring and is used for decoration.

Pargana was an administrative area comprising many villages and several parganas comprised a district.

Pathan refers to the tribesmen inhabiting the 'North-West Frontier' region between present day Pakistan and Afghanistan. The term was applied to the rulers of Delhi Sultanate, though most of the dynasties were of Turkish origin.

Peepul is a large tree *(Ficus religiosa)* that resembles some species of poplar, like the aspen. Its leaves constantly quiver in the breeze and its shade is very much sought after in hot summer days. The Buddha is said to have attained his enlightenment under one of these trees. The word came to English from Hindi. In Bengali the tree is called *ashwattha or ashath.*

Phalgun is the eleventh month of the Bengali calendar and the first spring month from mid-February to mid-March.

Purabi is a raga or mood in Indian classical music.

Sachi is the consort of Indra, the of the gods.

Santhal are important tribal people living in West Bengal and Bihar. They are noted for their songs and dances, their homemade brews, keen aesthetic sense and festive spirit.

Sari is the main part of a woman's dress in north India, draped around the body and then thrown over the head and shoulder.

Shal is a large tree valued for its timber and resin. Its leaves are used as disposable plates.

Shephali is a fragrant white flower blossoming in autumn.

Shindhu baroa is a raga in the classical Indian music.

Shisu is a large deciduous tree yielding valuable timbre. Its withered flowers hang from the branches for a long time and its seed-pods rustle in the wind.

Shiva is the third deity of the Hindu trinity of gods and one of the most important one with many roles and aspects. He is the destroyer, the supreme ascetic and meditative yogi. He is also the Hindu Mother Goddess (variously named as Parvati, Durga, Kali, etc.)

Sraban is the fourth month of the Bengali calendar from mid-July to mid-August and is the second month of the rainy season.

Tulsi is basil plant or its leaves

Urvashi is the most beautiful celestial nymph and dancer in the court of Indra, the king of the gods. The poem is based on the legend that Urvashi rose from the ocean. When the sea was churned with mount Mandar as the churning rod and the serpent Vasuki as the churning rope. She had in her one hand a chalice of nectar and in the other a chalice of poison. Lord Siva drank the poison to save all and his neck became blue. All the gods drank the nectar and became immortal.

Valmiki is said to be the first poet and the composer of the epic, the Ramayana. The legend has it that he was a robber in his early life and had a transformation through the grace of Saraswati, the goddess of learning and became a sage after years of austere practice. He was so moved to see a pair of birds, in loving embrace, being shot by a hunter's arrow that a beautiful couplet in Sanskrit came from his lips. That was the first poetry.

Veena is a string instrument, similar to sitar. Often poets use it as a metaphor for heart-string.

Index

First line of poem in Bengali

First Line	*Page*

First line of poem in English

First Line	*Page*

Key to Transliteration

অ	আ [া]	ই [ি]	ঈ [ী]	উ [ু]	ঊ [ূ]	ঋ [ৃ]
a	ā	i	ī	u	ū	rh

এ [ে]	ঐ [ৈ]	ও [ো]	ঔ [ৌ]	ং	ঃ
e	oi	o	oū	ṅ	ḥ

ক	খ	গ	ঘ	ঙ	চ	ছ	জ	ঝ	ঞ	ট	ঠ	ড	ঢ
k	kh	g	gh	ng	c	ch	j	jh	ñ	ṭ	ṭh	ḍ	ḍh

ঢ়	ণ	ত	থ	দ	ধ	ন	প	ফ	ব	ভ	ম	য	য়
ḍh	ṇ	t	th	d	dh	n	p	ph	b	bh	m	ẏ	y

র	ল	শ	ষ	স	হ	ক্ষ	ঁ
r	l	ś	ṣ	s	ḥ	kṣ	m̐